How to cook
fresh vegetables
simply nowadays

Original concept, photographs, template, illustrations: Chronoprint Publications
Authors : Annabelle Delaval & Arnold Weislo
With kind participation of Johan Sobry

Edition 2007
Printed in EU
ISBN No: 978-2-9529842-0-1

Nearly 100 recipes for 4 people, easy to make,
to discover the pleasure of fresh vegetables and healthy food on a daily basis.

What can you do with leeks? How can you prepare them? What's a courgette? How do you peel and cook it?

"Hi , I'd like to buy some fennel, I read it was good for the heart..."What does it look like? Do I have to cook it? For how long? What can I eat it with? And what about pumpkins? Can you eat them or are they just for Halloween decorations? Do they taste good? Eat vegetables...Yes, but no one taught me how to prepare them.

Eating healthy means having fruit and vegetables in our plate. We keep a lasting memory of meals tenderly prepared by our parents or friends, but if we don't know anything about vegetables, what should we do?

" *I must admit that myself being ignorant about vegetables, I felt totally helpless in farmers markets. Every time I went there with a friend of mine who happens to be a very good cook, I admired the ease with which he would compose his menus taking advantage of seasonal produce and promotions.*

Eat fresh vegetables to be in a good health ! I wrote this book to be as simple as possible, with a maximum of pictures, giving advice and tricks for all of the ninety five easy to realise and tasty recipes.

My friend Yohan Sobry, father of two teenagers, CEO and world champion of sand yachting and my girlfriend Abel, sculptor, who re-invents traditional cooking with creativity and simplicity, initiated me to their knowledge. They gave me the proof that in spite of limited time, with a very reasonable budget, without being a "Chef", it was easy to cook excellent dishes and eat healthily .

The Nutrition Department of the Institut Pasteur (Lille, France) approved my project. They specified the nutritional quality of each vegetable (calories, preservation, origins...) We elaborated all these recipes in a simple and educational way. All the pictures you see in the book actually present the result you will get.

"How to cook fresh vegetables simply nowadays" : give this book to people who are not used to cooking regularly. They will discover the simplicity of good eating."

Bon appétit ! "

Arnold Weislo.

NATURE IS GENEROUS

Fruits and vegetables are **naturally rich in vitamins, fibres, minerals and substances known as antioxidants.** The latter are for example vitamin C, E, coloured pigments found in certain fruits and vegetables (carotenes) or certain trace elements like selenium or zinc. Recent research clearly shows that **antioxidants are vital for the health of our cells.**

Vitamins take part in numerous **metabolic reactions.** The body cannot produce them in sufficient quantities. This is why vitamins must be taken as part of our diet.

Fibres are important to help intestinal transit. They do so **without contributing a high number of calories and quickly satiate the appetite.** Finally, they help to maintain good health by means of other mechanisms **(reduction of cholesterol, effects on intestinal bacteria…).**

These benefits help the body **to stay healthy naturally.** Fruits and vegetables have been attributed an important role in the **prevention of certain cancers and cardiovascular diseases.**

Such qualities have led nutritionists to make simple recommendations concerning the consumption of fruits and vegetables.

Consume 5 portions of fruits and vegetables everyday.

Fruits and vegetables contain many benefits for good health… but they can lose this if badly prepared. In fact, adding fat can increase the calories of such preparations. Here are some tips and hints which will help to reduce the amount of fat:

| **Avoid** cooking vegetables with butter, it is preferable to cook with none, or little fat (steam, oven-cook, microwave, grill…) | In most of the recipes in this book **low fat** cream can be used in the place of traditional cream. | To grease a dish or ramekin, use **oil** rather than butter. | Streaky bacon can be replaced with diced **ham.** |

Contents

Recipes are for 4 people

Tomatoes

PREPARATION

1 Chop...

2 Peel...

3 Scoop...

into cubes or cut
in round slices.

Put the tomatoes into boiling water for
1 minute, remove with a fork and peel off the skin.

slice off the top
of the tomato and scoop
out the seeds using a
small spoon.

TOMATOES, A VEGETABLE WITH 'HEART'

TOMATOES

water	proteins	carbohydrates	vitamin C	carotenes	fats
93,8 g	0,8 g	3,5 g	15 mg	600 µg	0,3 g

Average nutritional composition
of raw tomatoes (for 100g)

ORIGINS AND PRODUCTION

The tomato is a fruit which originally came from South America. They arrived in Europe during the 16th century starting with Italy, then Spain, and finally France and Britain. The tomato plant was first classed as an ornamental plant.

Today it is cultivated around the world with China being the leading producer. In Britain tomatoes are mostly cultivated in greenhouses and the rest is imported from Spain and the Canary Islands.

The tomato is a fruit of varying sizes, colours and shapes. In fact although some tomatoes weigh only a few grams, some can weigh up to 2kg! We find tomatoes of different colours such as yellow, red, orange, green, violet… They can be round, long, in the shape of a heart or a pear…

In Britain, tomatoes are better in **summer** when it is the harvest season. It is the best time to buy them as they are consequently less expensive.

NUTRITIONAL QUALITIES

Tomatoes are rich in water so they are very low in calories (19kcal in 100g). Consequently they contain few proteins, carbohydrates and fats. However they are rich in vitamin C and E and carotene.

HEALTH BENEFITS

Lycopene is a carotene that is found in fresh tomatoes but in higher quantities in tomato puree. It is better absorbed when the tomato is raw. Studies have found that tomatoes contains a component which provides cardiovascular protection.

Tomatoes contain an important amount of vitamin C, especially when raw, which helps fight against infections.

Information from the service of nutrition at the Institut Pasteur in Lille.

CHOOSING AND PRESERVING TOMATOES

Summer

The immense variety of tomatoes offers a diverse range of tastes. The acidity can be reduced by adding certain other varieties like the cherry tomatoes, for a more marked taste. Unfortunately these types of tomatoes tend to be more expensive than the majority commonly found.
Tomatoes taste better when eaten while red and if left out of the fridge in a place not too dry.
When they are cooked, the skin may be disagreeable but it is easy to remove the skin before use by leaving the tomatoes in boiling water for about 30 seconds.

Prawn
filled canapés
with Tomatoes

Use cherry tomatoes or any other type but round-shaped.

Wash, cut off the top, scoop out the inside with a small spoon and fill with small prawns mixed with a little mayonnaise.

The cherry tomatoes can be filled with crumbled goats cheese or tuna garnished with some black olives.

Tomatoes
and mozzarella

Remove the stalk and cut into round slices. Drain the buffalo mozzarella and slice. **Alternate the slices of cheese** with the tomatoes on a plate and **sprinkle with some finely chopped basil.**

Pour over a little olive oil and season with salt and pepper.

Add the juice of half a lemon or a little balsamic vinegar. Decorate with basil leaves and grated parmesan.

Stuffed
Tomatoes

Ingredients

250ml milk
salt/pepper
1 bunch of parsley
8 tomatoes
200g veal mince
1/2 onion
200g pork mince
3 garlic cloves
1 egg
100g bread

Wash the tomatoes.
Butter an oven proof dish.
Cut the top of each tomato and then scoop out the seeds by using a **teaspoon** making sure not to damage the skin. Place in the dish.

For the filling: warm the milk and **pour over the bread** which has been roughly crumbled. Leave to absorb. Peel the onion and garlic and wash the parsley. Chop all three ingredients finely. Whisk an egg and pour over the bread and mix in the minced meat, the onion, garlic and parsley and season to taste.
Place the tomato dish in the oven at 180°C.

Leave to cook for 30 to 45mins until the tomatoes have softened.

Serve hot. **The tomato pulp can be transformed into a sauce:** mix the flesh, add a trickle of olive oil, salt, pepper and some fresh basil leaves. **Cook** in a small casserole dish for a **few minutes. Serve the sauce with the stuffed tomatoes and white rice.**

Tomatoes and Goats Cheese Tart

Preparation : 15 mins
Cooking : 20 mins

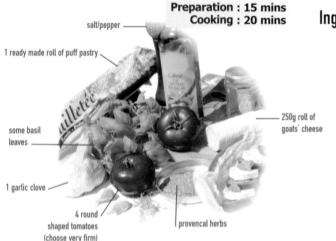

- salt/pepper
- 1 ready made roll of puff pastry
- some basil leaves
- 1 garlic clove
- 4 round shaped tomatoes (choose very firm)
- provencal herbs
- 250g roll of goats' cheese

Roll out the puff pastry into a pastry tin. Cut the tomatoes and goats cheese into round slices. Cover the puff pastry with alternate slices of both and sprinkle over the provencal herbs and salt and pepper.

Cook in the oven for 20 minutes at 180°C. The tart should cook slowly (the puff pastry should not blacken around the edges). Serve with a mixed salad.

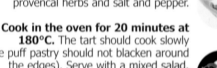

Tomato Spaghetti Sauce

Preparation : 10 mins
Cooking : 20 mins

Ingredients

- 15 green olives
- 4-6 tomatoes
- provencal herbs
- 1 sprig of thyme
- 2 garlic cloves
- 1 onion
- spaghetti
- salt/pepper
- Olive oil

(If you have prepared the stuffed tomatoes you can use the pulp for the sauce).

Peel the tomatoes. Cut into small pieces. Finely chop the olives. Brown the sliced onion with a little olive oil for 5 minutes. Add the tomatoes, salt, pepper and the sprig of thyme.

Leave to cook on low heat for 20 minutes, mixing occasionally. To have a more smooth effect the sauce can be blended.

This sauce (without the olives) is the base of different robust tomato sauces to which you can add the spices of your choice.

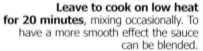

Aubergines

PREPARATION

1 Trim
2 Chop
3 Scoop out seeds
4 Salt
5 Wipe

cut the stalk and leaves of the aubergine.

according to your needs in either round slices, cubes or strips.

leave the chopped aubergine covered with sea salt for about 1 hour (this stops excess absorption of oil during cooking) - Wipe: Before cooking wipe off the salt from the aubergines with absorbent paper.

AUBERGINES COMBATS AGAINST HIGH CHOLESTEROL !

AUBERGINES

energy	water	fibres	carbohydrates	proteins
18 kcal	92,2 g	2,5 g	3,5 g	0,9 g

Average nutritional composition of aubergines (for 100g)

ORIGINS AND PRODUCTION

The aubergine is a fruit from the family solanaceae, it is closely related to tomatoes and potatoes. The fruit is picked and cooked before it reaches full maturity.

Originally from India, where even today we find many varieties, the cultivation of aubergines in Europe started in Italy during the 15th century. It's only after two centuries that the growth of this vegetable spread to France. It is cultivated in the south from **May to October.** The rest of the year it is imported from the West Indies, Israel and Senegal.

Aubergines are more suited to temperate climates and so are grown in green houses in Britain.

The aubergine has never been widely consumed in Britain even though it is the 9th most eaten vegetable in the world. In recent years the trend has changed thanks to the increasing popularity of a Mediterranean diet resulting in an increase in consumption.

NUTRITIONAL QUALITIES

Low in calories since it is full of water; the aubergine contains a high density of nutrients (minerals, fibres and vitamins).
With just 18 Kcal in 100g, it is placed on the same level as the cucumber, chicory and lettuce.

HEALTH BENEFITS

Studies carried out in the USA and Austria show that the fibres found in aubergines help eliminate fats and cholesterol in the blood by limiting their absorption by the intestine.

Information from the service of nutrition at the Institut Pasteur in Lille.

CHOOSING AND PRESERVING THE AUBERGINE

May to October

An aubergine with unblemished, taut and lustrous skin, a deep violet colour and a bright green stalk end, will be ready to be eaten. If the vegetable becomes too mature the colour reddens and the skin becomes bitter.
Aubergines can be kept in the refrigerator for up to a week in the vegetable compartment.

Grilled Aubergines

salt/pepper

olive oil

3 aubergines

4 garlic cloves minced

parsley chopped

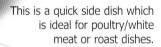

Cut the aubergines in round slices of about 1cm thickness. After leaving them to salt, wipe them and **pan fry them gently in a little olive oil.** Season with salt and pepper and leave to cook for about 1 minute on each side. Place the softened slices into a serving dish and **sprinkle with some finely chopped garlic and parsley**

This is a quick side dish which is ideal for poultry/white meat or roast dishes.

Aubergine Ragu

Ingredients

1 tbsp olive oil

1 jar bolognese sauce (good quality)

1 ball of buffalo mozzarella

6 small aubergines

50g parmesan

salt/pepper

2 tbsp flour

Slice the 6 aubergines lengthways without peeling them. **After covering them with salt and wiping them, cover them lightly on both sides with flour** and **pan fry the slices** in a little olive oil. Next, drain them by placing on some absorbent paper.

In a roasting dish cover the base with the aubergine slices. **Alternate** one layer of **aubergines** with slices of **mozzarella** and season with salt and pepper. Finish by covering with the Bolognese sauce and with grated parmesan (or you can make parmesan shavings using a potato peeler).

Roast in the oven for maximum 15mins (until the cheese melts and turns golden) at **180°C.**

Serve with rocket salad seasoned with a little lemon juice and olive oil.

Moussaka

Preparation : 20 mins
Cooking : 10 mins + 45 mins

olive oil

salt/pepper

500ml milk

3 aubergines

30g flour

2 onions

2 tomatoes

500g minced lamb

ground coriander
mozzarella (optional)
30g butter
some breadcrumbs

Parmesan
(optional)

Make the béchamel sauce by melting the butter in a pan. Add the flour and cook by adding milk and season with salt.

Remove the stalks and cut the aubergines lengthways in 5mm thick slices. Grill or pan fry the slices (if doing the latter leave on absorbent paper after), 1 minute on each side and then season each slice with salt.

Peel and roughly cut the onions and brown them with some oil in a pot. **Add the mince** and cook for 5mins. Peel and **add the tomatoes**, season with salt, pepper and some ground coriander.

Place a fine layer of breadcrumbs at the bottom of an oven-proof dish and then add alternate **layers of aubergine, mince and the béchamel sauce.**

Finish with either a layer of slices of mozzarella, or the béchamel sauce, or with grated parmesan. Cook in the middle part of the **oven for** 45mins at **200°C** and serve with a mixed salad.

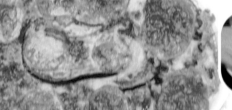

Aubergine 'Caviar'

Preparation : 15 mins
Cooking : 25/40 mins

Ingredients

salt/pepper

juice of 1 lemon

2 tbsp olive oil

10 coriander grains

2 aubergines

2 garlic cloves

Trim and wash the aubergines. Wrap whole in aluminium foil and bake in the oven for 25 to 40mins (depending on their size).

When cooked **remove from the oven** and cut in half.

With a small spoon scoop out the flesh (if the seeds are too big remove before scooping out the flesh).

Peel and crush the garlic cloves along with the coriander seeds and **add to the mixture of aubergines.**

Add the lemon juice and olive oil and mix well using a fork until smooth and creamy.

Serve warm with fish or grilled meat **or cold** on toasted bread to make tapas.

Peppers

PREPARATION

1 Core...
2 Cut...
3 Grill...
4 Peel...

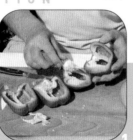
1

2

3

place the halved peppers for 10 minutes on a grill. Seal in a plastic bag for 5 minutes...

4

peeling will be easier

PEPPERS RICH IN VITAMIN C

PEPPERS

fibres 2 g	energy 25 kcal	proteins 0,9 g	carbohydrates 4,9 g	vitamin C 146 mg	fats 0,3 g

Average nutritional composition of raw peppers (for 100g)

ORIGINS AND PRODUCTION

Peppers (or capsicums) are originally from South America but can now be found in all of southern Europe.

China is the number one world producer but peppers are also grown in **Britain where they are harvested during summer.**

Its colour depends on its maturity and also on the species. Peppers exist as yellow, green, red, purple, orange…

Peppers are part of the capsicum family which includes sweet peppers or bell peppers, which are mild in taste and also many hotter varieties such as chilli peppers.

NUTRITIONAL QUALITIES

The pepper contains very few calories: it contains little fat, protein and carbohydrates but it contains a lot of water. Its energy value is weak (25kcal)

It has a high concentration of vitamin C, carotenes (responsible for its colour) and fibres.

In fact the high quantity of vitamin C places the pepper at number two after parsley. In some cases the level can be up to 300mg for every 100g depending on the variety and maturity of the vegetable, in other words 5 times the level found in an orange.

HEALTH BENEFITS

The richness of fibres in peppers makes this vegetable an important digestive aid. Vitamin C and carotenes are important anti-oxidants which can help protect against heart disease and some cancers.

Information from the service of nutrition at the Institut Pasteur in Lille.

Summer

CHOOSING AND PRESERVING PEPPERS

The pepper should be chosen firm and smooth, with an unblemished and lustrous skin.

It can be kept in the vegetable compartment in the fridge or in a cold place for up to a week. If left at room temperature it will dry and wrinkle.

The skin can be easily removed by grilling it in the oven. This is ideal in the case of digestive problems.

Fish Parcels with Peppers and Vegetables

Preparation : 20 mins
Cooking : 20 mins + 30 mins

4 peppers
salt/pepper
dill (+ other herbs)
1 large onion
600g white fish
some white wine
2 carrots

Peel the carrots and **cut** into round slices. **Core, deseed and chop the peppers** into cubes (you can also grill and peel the peppers before chopping to give an even better taste). **Brown the onion** in some olive oil. **Add the carrots** and leave to cook for 10 minutes mixing occasionally (some white wine can also be added).

Add the chopped peppers. Continue the cooking for 10 minutes stirring continuously and season with salt and pepper. **Place a bed of vegetables on some aluminium foil** (35cm). Put a piece of fish on top. Add a sprig of dill or thyme. Add **2 tablespoons of white wine** and close the aluminium foil to form a parcel.

Place in the oven (200°C) for approximately 30 minutes. When the parcel inflates: it's done! The parcels can be prepared a few hours in advance and left in the fridge until cooked.

Stuffed Peppers

Preparation : 15 mins
Cooking : 10 mins + 40 mins

Ingredients

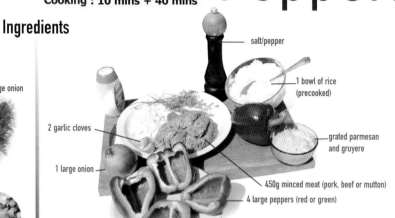

salt/pepper
1 bowl of rice (precooked)
2 garlic cloves
grated parmesan and gruyere
1 large onion
450g minced meat (pork, beef or mutton)
4 large peppers (red or green)

Cut the peppers in half; remove the stalk, core and seeds. Do not pee[l] Rinse. **Mix the chopped onion** with the mince. Add salt and peppe[r] (chopped parsley can also be mixed in). **Add the parmesan, rice an[d] the garlic** crushed. **Fill each half of the pepper** with the mixture[.]

Sprinkle over the grated gruyere. Decorate with a round slice of pepper of a different colour to the pepper filled. **Cook in the middle of the oven** (180°C) for about 1 hour. (to reduce the cooking time the halved peppers can be left in boiling water for about 3 minutes before being filled. In this case, the cooking time in the oven will be reduced to 40 minutes).

Provençal Sauce with Peppers

Preparation : 20 mins
Cooking : 15 mins max

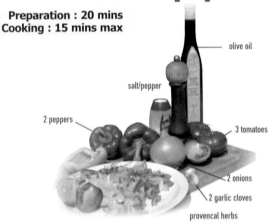

- olive oil
- salt/pepper
- 2 peppers
- 3 tomatoes
- 2 onions
- 2 garlic cloves
- provencal herbs

Chop all the vegetables in small pieces.
Brown the onions first in some olive oil (on low heat).
Add the chopped peppers and **tomatoes.**
Stir continuously. Season to taste with salt and pepper. Add the herbs.

Continue cooking until the tomatoes are completely dissolved. The sauce can be thinned by increasing the amount of tomatoes added.

You can also use tomato pulp of good quality (not concentrate!).

Peppers with Olive Oil

Preparation : 20 mins
Cooking : 15 mins (to remove skin)

Ingredients

- olive oil
- 4 peppers
- provencal herbs
- salt/pepper

After grilling the 4 peppers in the oven for 10 minutes, **remove the skin. Cut the peppers in wide strips** of 3cm width. Place in a clear dish by mixing the colours of the peppers and sprinkling with the herbs.

Pour over some olive oil until the peppers are completely covered. **Cover and keep in the fridge** for at least 24 hours. This dish can be used as tapas or can be served alongside fish or grilled white meat. It will keep for a few days if stored in the fridge.

Roasted Red Pepper Sauce

Preparation : 10 mins
Cooking : 10 mins

Cut the stalks of the peppers. Halve them and clear out the seeds. **Grill for 10 minutes in order to peel** off the skin. Chop the peppers. Peel the garlic and onion and **brown the chopped garlic in some oil**. Add the peppers and mix. Leave on low heat for 5 minutes. Away from the heat **mix the peppers and then reheat for 5 minutes.** This sauce can be used hot on white fish or cold as an accompaniment to grilled vegetables, decorated with basil leaves.

17

Courgettes

PREPARATION

1 Peel...

2 Chop...

3 Slice...

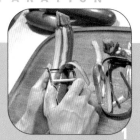

COURGETTES, THE EYE-SIGHT PROTECTOR

COURGETTES

water 94 g	proteins 1,8 g	carbohydrates 2 g	**vitamin C** 20 mg	fats 0,2 g

Average nutritional composition of raw courgettes (for 100g)

ORIGINS AND PRODUCTION

The courgette comes from Central America where it has been cultivated for centuries. It is much appreciated by the habitants of the Mediterranean.

Once considered a delicacy, they are now a popular choice in Britain. Although they are available all year round they are of better quality and cheaper in summer.

There are many varieties of courgettes which can be distinguished by their form and colour. The most common is the green variety which has a long oblong shape. It can also be found as round and green, white, yellow and even grey.

NUTRITIONAL QUALITIES

Courgettes contain a high level of water but have low levels of proteins, sugars and fats. This vegetable is very low in calories (17kcal/100g).
The amount of vitamin C is high, especially if the courgette is eaten raw.
The content of fibres is not very high but increase as the courgette mature.
Potassium is the mineral of highest quantity.
It is a good source of lutein, a naturally occurring carotene.

HEALTH BENEFITS

Courgette is good for health because of its minerals, trace elements, vitamins and fibres and its low level of calories.

Lutein is vital for the eyes.

Like most vegetable, it is important for a balanced nutritional diet.

Information from the service of nutrition at the Institut Pasteur in Lille.

CHOOSING AND PRESERVING COURGETTES

June to October

British production is from **June to October**. Courgettes should be chosen for their firm and shiny skin, green and unblemished. It is tender when consumed young and can be kept for 4-5 days in dry and cold place..

Courgette, Tarragon and Parmesan Veloute

Preparation : 10 mins
Cooking : 10 mins + 5 mins

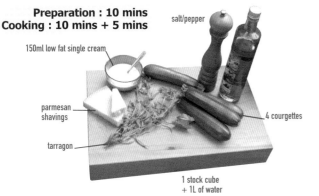

- salt/pepper
- 150ml low fat single cream
- parmesan shavings
- tarragon
- 4 courgettes
- 1 stock cube + 1L of water

Chop the courgettes into small pieces. Season with salt and pepper and **steam** for 10 minutes. **Bring the stock mixture to boil.**
Pick the tarragon leaves and mince them finely. **Blend the cooked courgettes** in a blender. **Add the stock** and the **minced tarragon.** Pour the mixture into a pot, **add 1 tbsp of olive oil** and leave to cook on low heat. **Pour in the cream** and **cook for 5 minutes.** Serve in bowls. Decorate with **some tarragon leaves** and **parmesan shavings.**

Courgette and Mint Salad

Ingredients

Preparation : 10 mins
Cooking : 10 mins

- salt/pepper
- 2 green courgettes
- 2 yellow courgettes
- 2 tbsp olive oil
- juice of 1 lemon + chilli or herbs to season
- 5 mint sprigs

Steam the courgettes (washed) without peeling and chopped, for 10 minutes. **Leave to cool in a plate. Finely mince** the mint and **sprinkle** over the courgettes. **Pour over the lemon juice,** and 2tbsp **olive oil.** Add salt and pepper to taste.

Serve chilled.

Courgette and Coriander Tortilla

Preparation : 10 mins
Cooking : 10 mins

salt/pepper

50g parmesan grated or shavings

2 courgettes

8 eggs

5 strands of coriander

Peel and grate 2 courgettes. Cook in a pan for 5 minutes in some olive oil. **Chop the coriander. Whisk the eggs.** Add salt and pepper to taste. **Add the coriander.** Mix. Pour this mixture on to the courgettes in the pan. **Mix.**

Leave to cook for 10 minutes on low heat. Flip over to cook both sides till golden.

Sprinkle over the parmesan shavings.

Courgette Tagliatelle

Ingredients

Preparation : 25 mins
Cooking : 2 mins

2 eggs
1 box of breadcrumbs
3 courgettes
olive oil

Peel and slice the courgettes lengthways (with a potato peeler). **Whisk the eggs** and add salt and pepper to taste.

Place some breadcrumbs in a plate. Heat some olive oil in a pan. **Dip the slices** in the egg mixture and then in the breadcrumbs.

Cook till golden in the pan for about 1 minute on each side. Add some oil between each batch (keep the cooked courgettes warm in the oven). Once cooked, place the cooked strips on absorbent paper.

This dish can be eaten hot or cold as tapas, why not pour over some lemon juice?

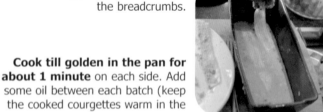

Chicory
or french endive

PREPARATION

1 Remove leaves...

2 Chop...

1 remove the outer leaves if they are not white. Cut the base of the chicory. Remove its core (as it can make the vegetable bitter during cooking)

2 wash the chicory under cold running water. Cut in half for more rapid cooking. Cut in round slices for salads.

CHICORY
or french endive

ORIGINS AND PRODUCTION

There exist some varieties that come from wild chicory that the Egyptians used to eat. Those that we know today, long-shaped and white and pale yellow coloured appeared in Belgium in the 19th century under the name of witloof meaning 'white leaves'. At this time chicory had a very bitter taste but after selection and improvement the plant has achieved a milder taste. A few years later it could be found in British grocers.

France is the leading producer and the chicory (or French endive) is mostly cultivated in the north where it named the 'pearl of the north'.

In Italy, we find a red coloured endive 'la Carmina' which is a cross between the white endive and red chicory.

fibres	water	proteins	carbohydrates	vitamine C	fats
2,5 g	94,7 g	1 g	0,7 g	5 mg	0,2 g

Average nutritional composition of raw chicory (for 100g)

NUTRITIONAL QUALITIES

Chicory contains a lot of water, few carbohydrates, proteins and fats. It is therefore low in calories (8kcal/100g). However, it has an important level of fibres and selenium.

HEALTH BENEFITS

Selenium is a trace element which is gaining importance with researchers. It works as an antioxidant and slows the ageing of cells. It may also play an important role against certain cancers.

Information from the service of nutrition at the Institut Pasteur in Lille.

CHOOSING AND PRESERVING CHICORY

October to May

Chicory are harvested from **October to May.** It is therefore preferable to eat this vegetable during winter. When choosing chicory look for tightly closed leaves that are not wilting. Chicory classified in category II and III may have slightly green leaves and will be slightly bitter. This bitterness can be reduced during cooking by adding sugar.

Chicory should be kept away from light to prevent it becoming green and bitter. In the refrigerator, it can be kept for 6 days enveloped in absorbent paper.

Chicory and Ham Gratin

Preparation : 20 mins
Cooking : 10 mins + 15 mins

- 500ml milk
- salt/pepper
- 50g grated gruyere
- 1 slice of ham per person
- 25g butter
- 2 tbsp flour
- 1 chicory per person

Cook the chicory cut in two, 10 minutes in boiling salted water.
Prepare a 'roux': melt 25g butter in a pot. When it starts to bubble add 2 tbsp of flour. Stir rapidly with a whisk. When the lumps start to dry, gradually add the 500ml of milk (or 250ml milk and 250ml water from the cooked vegetable) whisking continuously.
Mix and **leave to cook** gently for a few minutes until the sauce thickens. Season with pepper. On a board **wrap 2 chicory halves** in a **ham slice** to make a roll. Place the rolls into an **oven-proof dish** and **cover with the white sauce.** Sprinkle over the cheese and **cook in the oven at 180° C for 15 minutes.**

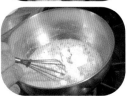

Tip: cheese lovers can add some grated gruyere into the sauce while it is still hot before pouring it into the dish.

Chicken and Chicory curry

Preparation : 20 mins
Cooking : 8 mins

Ingredients

- salt/pepper
- low fat single cream
- 2 chicken fillets
- 1 tbsp olive oil
- 2 tsp curry powder
- 4 endives

Cut the chicory in half, core and cut in small pieces. **Chop the chicken fillets** into small cubes. Brown the chicken in a pan with some olive oil. Add the chicory, salt and pepper.

Sprinkle in the curry powder. Leave to cook on gentle heat for 5 minutes.
Pour over some **cream.**
Leave for a few minutes on gentle heat and then serve immediately.

Tip: decorate each plate with some fine slices of raw chicory.

Complete Salad with Chicory

**Preparation : 5 mins
No cooking**

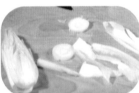

1 thick slice of ham chopped

3 endives

Comté or mature cheddar cheese

oil, vinegar
Salt/pepper

1 apple

parsley

walnuts

Ingredients

Mix pieces of chicory, washed, with the apple, ham and Comté cut into cubes.

Make vinaigrette with 3 tbsp olive oil, 1 tbsp vinegar, salt and pepper.

Add crushed nuts.
Mix and serve immediately.

Roasted Chicory

Accompaniment of meat
(lamb or veal ribs)

Cut the chicory in half and brown in a pot with some butter and oil. Add salt and pepper, stir. Leave it to cook covered on low heat for 15 minutes while, checking all the time. The chicory should be soft, but pay attention not to let them it burn.

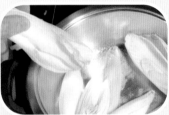

NB: you can eventually remove some of the bitterness if you feel it is necessary (taste halfway through) by adding a tsp of sugar.

Simple !

Chicory salad
To suit all tastes !

Cut the chicory in round slices and wash under a tap.
Dry with absorbent paper. **Mix with one tbsp of mayonnaise** (or a mixture made up of half mayonnaise and half fat fromage frais). Serve as a side dish.

Chicory Canapés

Separate the chicory leaves and wash them with cold water. Pour over lemon juice to stop them colouring. Fill each leaf with a filling of your choice: **crab, prawns, roquefort...**

Spinach

PREPARATION

1 Cut...

2 Blanch...

remove stalks and roughly cut. Wash several
times in cold water.

plunge the spinach in a large pot full of
boiling salted water for 5 minutes.
NB: after cooking, spinach reduces
to half its volume.

SPINACH

fibres	vitamin B9	calcium	carotenes	vitamin C	iron
3 g	140 µg	112 mg	4460 µg	10 mg	2,4 mg

Nutritional composition of cooked spinach (for 100g)

ORIGINS AND PRODUCTION

Spinach probably originates from Iran or Afghanistan. It was probably introduced to Europe through Andalusia by the Moors, little before the 1st century.

A cookbook belonging to King Richard II demonstrates that spinach was grown in England in the 14th century.

It was grown in France thanks to Catherine de Medicis a historical figure in the 16th century. When she left her home in Florence to marry the king of France, she brought along her own cooks, who could prepare spinach the ways that she especially liked. Since this time, dishes prepared on a bed of spinach are referred to as "a la Florentine".

China is the leading producer of spinach. The varieties found in the garden may be different to those cultivated for commerce: we find 'Giant Winter', 'Dominant', 'Space' and even 'Trinidad'.

NUTRITIONAL QUALITIES

Spinach is a vegetable low in protein, carbohydrates and fats but rich in water. It is therefore low in calories (18kcal/100g).
It is high in nutrients such as vitamins C, E, B9 (folic acid), fibres, carotenes (particularly lutein), calcium and iron.
It is also the source of Omega 3 making it a good source of nutrients.

HEALTH BENEFITS

For pregnant women, folic acid limits the risk of malformation of the closing of the spinal cord in the foetus called Spina Bifida. The provitamin A and vitamin C and E plays a protective role against certain cancers. Its high level of lutein is beneficial for preventing the age-related degeneration of eyesight.

Iron fights against anaemia. It is better absorbed by the body when the vegetable is eaten with Vitamin C, for example with citrus fruits.

Information from the service of nutrition at the Institut Pasteur in Lille.

CHOOSING AND PRESERVING SPINACH

Fresh spinach is smooth and dark green. It can only be kept for two days in the vegetable compartment in the fridge. It is better to cook the day of purchase. It is possible to freeze after blanching the spinach for 3 minutes in boiling water, drained.

Spinach and Salmon Tarte

Ingredients

2 rolls of ready-made puff pastry

salt/pepper

500g salmon

700g fresh spinach

150g gorgonzola

After **blanching the spinach** squeeze out the water by pressing it down in a sieve. **Cut** the **salmon** and **gorgonzola** into large cubes

Place the puff pastry into a tart tin. Spread the salmon, gorgonzola and the spinach on top. **Re-cover** the dish with the **second roll of puff pastry** and close the edges firmly.

The puff pastry can be covered with some egg yolk to give a more golden coloured effect.

Bake in the oven for 25 minutes at 200°C.

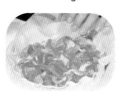

Spinach and Ham Soufflé

1kg fresh spinach

30g butter

3 eggs

salt/pepper

150g ham

50g grated gruyere

1 chicken stock cube mixed with 100ml of boiling water

grated nutmeg

1 tbsp flour

Cook 1kg of spinach in salted boiling water for 5 minutes and puree it using a blender.

Dry the spinach on low heat with 30g butter, add 1 tbsp of flour, salt, pepper, nutmeg, and the boiling stock, leave to cook on very low heat for 10 minutes.

Once removed from the heat, mix in 50g grated cheese with 150g cooked ham, 3 egg yolks and whipped egg whites. Place in a buttered mould and leave to cook in a preheated oven at 200°C for 35 minutes.

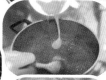

Spinach à la Florentine

Preparation : 20 mins
Cooking : 10 mins

Ingredients

- salt/pepper
- 4 tbsp low fat crème fraîche
- 4 eggs
- potato puree (for 4 people)
- 50g grated gruyere
- 2.5kg fresh spinach
- grated nutmeg

Prepare the spinach puree: cook the spinach in salted boiling water for 5 minutes. Drain and press then puree in a blender.

...pare a potato puree with 6 medium size potatoes ...e potato section). Place the hot puree in the base of an ...n-proof dish.

...h a large tbsp press down to form ...r wells in the puree and fill with the ...s, season with pepper. **Cover with ...hot spinach, leaving the egg ...ks visible.**

...e a tsp of crème fraîche over each ...yolk. **Sprinkle over the grated ...yere and place in the oven for ...minutes at 200°C.**

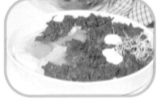

Spinach and Ricotta Cake

Preparation : 15 mins
Cooking : 5 mins + 40 mins

- some nutmeg and dill
- salt/pepper
- 1kg fresh spinach
- 2tbsp flour
- tomatoes (for the sauce)
- 200ml low fat single cream
- 3 eggs
- 300g ricotta

Cook the fresh spinach and then chop. **Squeeze the spinach against a sieve to remove the maximum of water.** Season with salt and pepper. Whisk the eggs and the cream together and season with dill and nutmeg. **Add the flour to the spinach.** Mix lightly but smoothly the chopped spinach, egg/crème mixture and the ricotta. Place in a non-stick rectangular cake tin and cook in the oven at 180°C for 40 minutes. Leave to cool a little bit and then carefully remove from the mould. For the tomato sauce see the tomato page (spaghetti sauce).

Tip: it can be eaten cold with a sauce of chopped tomatoes and some basil or warm with some fresh goat's cheese.

29

Pumpkins

PREPARATION

1 Scoop out the
   seeds...

2 Peel...

3 Chop...

| Fibres 1,3 g | Provitamin A 2 mg | Proteins 0,8 g | carbohydrates 4,1 g | Vitamin C 7 mg | Fats 0,1 g |

Average nutritional composition of pumpkins (for 100g)

ORIGINS AND PRODUCTION

Pumpkins originally come from Central America. They arrived in Europe after the voyage of Christopher Columbus to America.

It is now grown in all hot countries and in cooler climates. The leading producer is China.

In Britain, it is mostly cultivated by three main producers in the south and is harvested at the beginning of autumn but is better suited to warmer climates. .

Pumpkins are easily confused with winter squash even through they are two different vegetables. We have however many varieties of pumpkin and they can range from small and light to record-breaking weights and sizes.

NUTRITIONAL QUALITIES

Pumpkins are vegetables which are low in calories (20kcal/100g) because they contain few proteins and fats.
Like all fresh vegetables it contains little sodium.

It contains a high concentration of provitamin A and practically all the vitamins found in group B.
In its skin there is a high number of trace elements (zinc, iodine, copper...)

HEALTH BENEFITS

Provitamin A possesses an anti-oxidant activity which protects against the ageing of cells.It also boosts the immune system.

Fibres contained in the pumpkin help intestinal digestion.

Its low level of sodium allows the pumpkin to be eaten by people on a low sodium diet.

Information from the service of nutrition at the Institut Pasteur in Lille.

CHOOSING AND PRESERVING PUMPKINS

October to December

Pumpkins are in season from **October** to the end of **December**.
It should be chosen when its stalk is full of sap and its skin is without blemishes, which indicate the presence of mould.
Smaller pumpkins are sweeter and contain less fibres.

Pumpkin Soup

Preparation : 15 mins
Cooking : 35 mins

- salt/pepper
- parsley and coriander chopped
- 300ml milk
- handful of rice
- 1.5kg pumpkin
- 30g butter or a little oil
- 1 tomato
- 1 onion
- 2tbsp low fat crème fraîche for the dressing (optional)
- + 750ml water

Peel the pumpkin and scoop out the seeds. **Cut into large cubes.** Peel and finely chop the onion. Peel and cut the tomato in large chunks. Brown the onions in a pot with some butter or oil.

Add the rice and leave to cook until the grains become slightly transparent. **Add the tomato chunks** and mix. Add the pumpkin pieces, salt, pepper and add the chopped coriander. Mix well. Pour in the milk and stir. Add the water; the pumpkin should be completely covered. **Cover and leave to cook for 30 minutes. Blend in a mixer**.

Serve in bowls and add 1 tsp of low fat crème fraîche and a little chopped parsley. To add to the flavour you can add half tsp of curry or cumin powder while still cooking.

Pumpkin Quiche

Preparation : 15 mins
Cooking : 10 mins + 35 mins

Ingredients
4 pers.

- 1 tbsp olive oil
- 1 tsp curry powder salt/pepper
- low fat crème fraîche
- 150g grated cheese
- 1 ready made roll of pastry
- 500g pumpkin
- 200g diced smoked streaky bacon
- 2 garlic cloves
- 2 onions

Peel and cut the pumpkins in large chunks. Cook in a pot with salted water for 10 minutes.

Drain well and then mash the pumpkin. If there still rests some water remove it by pressing down the puree.
Add the grated cheese and the low fat crème fraîche and mix.

Heat the oil in a pan and brown the chopped onions, when they become transparent add the crushed garlic and mix well. **Add the bacon and season with curry powder**. Mix. **Place the pastry in a tart case.** Spread the pumpkin puree over the pastry, add the bacon and onions. The tart can be decorated with some cumin seeds.
Bake in the oven for 35 minutes at 200°C.

Small Pumpkin Soufflé

Ingredients
4 pers.

- 4 small pumpkins
- salt/pepper
- 200ml milk
- 70g grated gruyere
- grated nutmeg
- 3tbsp flour
- 3 eggs
- 30g butter

① Cut off the lid of the pumpkin. Remove the seeds inside. Place the pumkins in a plate and cover with a sheet of aluminium foil.

② **Bake for 1 hour at 220°C.** Remove the pumpkins from the oven. Scoop out the flesh with a small spoon without cutting trough the skin. Mash the pulp with a fork.

③ **For the 'roux': melt the butter in a pot and add the flour.** Stir in the milk gradually, salt, pepper and add the nutmeg. Separate the yolk and whites of the eggs. **Add the yolks to the roux and mix.** Add the pumpkin pulp and the grated gruyere. **Whisk the egg whites until light and fluffy and fold them delicately into the mixture. Fill the pumpkins with the mixture,** sprinkle over some freshly grated nutmeg. Bake (about 20 minutes) at 220°C until the soufflés are golden. **Serve immediately.**

Tip : if your have some mixture left over your can cook it in a round dish.

Pumpkin Chips (tapas)

- 500g pumpkin
- 3cm oil in a deep pan
- salt
- salt/ powdered cumin to vary the flavour

A colourful variation on chips. Peel and cut the pumpkin in large chunks. Cut in the shape of chips by hand or with the **help of a machine.**

Heat the oil and fry the pumpkins for a few minutes or until they become golden.

Drain on some absorbent paper once cooked through.

Serve immediately and season with salt or powdered cumin.

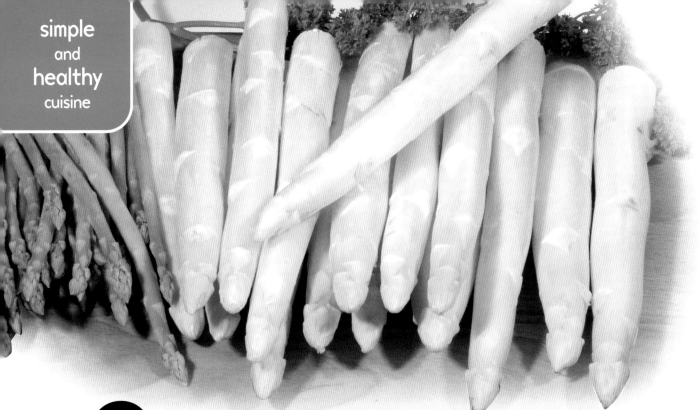

Asparagus

PREPARATION

1 Peel...

2 Chop...

1

peel white asparagus which will be used for soup with a potato peeler. The small green variety doesn't need to be peeled.

2

asparagus can be cooked by letting them boil flat in a pan filled with salted water. Once cooked the asparagus should be removed gently to prevent breaking them.

smart idea!

So that your dish tastes even better, cook the asparagus in the salted stock water... of the peelings!

ASPARAGUS, THE VEGETABLE FOR PREGNANT WOMEN!

ASPARAGUS

fibres	vitamin B9	proteins	carbohydrates	vitamin C	fats
1,3 g	110 µg	2,7 g	1,5 g	10 mg	0,3 g

Nutritional composition of cooked asparagus (for 100g)

ORIGINS AND PRODUCTION

Asparagus is a garden vegetable which comes from the heart of the Mediterranean. The Greeks and the Egyptians consumed wild asparagus and it was the Romans who cultivated it.

It has been grown in England since the 16th century (it is not widely cultivated anywhere else in the UK).

Asparagus is picked from **May** until the **end of June**. It is principally grown in Worcestershire, Lincolnshire and Kent.

We find green and white varieties of asparagus, the point can be green – purple if it is grown in the fresh air.

NUTRITIONAL QUALITIES

Rich in water and low in fats, proteins and carbohydrates, asparagus has few calories (19kcal/100g).

The quantity of vitamins varies depending on the variety. The amount of vitamin C remains high even after cooking.
It also has a high concentration of folic acid (vitamin B9).

HEALTH BENEFITS

Asparagus possess an important diuretic action. Its level of folic acid plays an important role in the correct development and closing of the spinal chord of a foetus during pregnancy : Spina Bifida.

The composition of fibres helps regulate intestinal transit without irritating the inner wall of the digestive tube.

Information from the service of nutrition at the Institut Pasteur in Lille.

May to end of June

CHOOSING AND PRESERVING ASPARAGUS

When buying, the stem should not be too dry. The leaves at the point or spear should be tight and the stem short. It can be kept in the fridge for one or two days maximum enveloped in a cloth which will serve to conserve it. It is also possible to freeze them after blanching.

Asparagus à la Flamande

Preparation : 15 mins
cooking : 10 mins + 20 mins

salt/pepper

4 eggs

50g butter

6-8 asparagus per person

a handful of prawns or parmesan shavings to decorate

Asparagus Soup

Preparation : 20 mins
Cooking : 10 mins + 20 mins

Ingredients

As a starter or main dish, after increasing the quantity, quick and easy.

salt/pepper

1 large box of white asparagus

1L water (or better 1/2 L milk and 1/2L asparagus stock)

100ml low fat single cream

some green asparagus spears

Peel the asparagus and boil the peelings in a large pot of boiling salted water for 10 minutes. **Remove them while keeping the flavoured water. Cook the asparagus whole** in the stock of peelings for 20 minutes (increase the cooking time if the asparagus are very large).

Hard boil the eggs for 10 minutes. **Shell** the eggs and **mash** them with the help of a fork. Gently melt the butter (place the butter in a bowl and place the bowl over a container filled with hot water).

Drain the asparagus and **place** length-ways in a plate. **Mix the melted butter** and the mashed eggs, **pour the mixture over the asparagus** and decorate with some prawns or with some parmesan shavings or with some parsley.

Peel the asparagus and **boil the peelings** in a large pot of boiling salted water for 10 minutes. Remove them while keeping the flavoured water. **Cut the asparagus** in 3cm length chunks and cook in the boiling stock for 20 minutes.

Blend the soup. Add the milk and cream, leave on low heat and stir every few minutes.

Add the green asparagus spears which have been 'poached' for a few minutes in salted boiling water.

Asparagus Flan with Orange sauce

Preparation : 25 mins
Cooking : 15 mins + 40 mins

- 1kg green asparagus
- juice of 1 orange
- salt/pepper
- saffron
- chervil
- 150ml low fat single cream + 2tbsp low fat crème fraîche
- 100g raw chicken fillet
- 2tsp corn flour
- some butter
- 4 eggs

Individually butter the ramekins. Peel the asparagus, **cut in chunks of 4cm,** and cook for 15 minutes in boiling salted water.
Refresh them under cold running water, leave them on absorbent paper. Keep the spears.

Break the eggs in to the bowl of a blender and add cream, corn flour, the chicken chopped into small pieces, the stalks of asparagus, salt, pepper and strands of chervil. **Blend until a smooth cream is obtained.**

Line the ramekins with the asparagus spears. Fill with the preparation and cover with some aluminium foil.
Cooking: bain-marie in the oven at 160°C, 40 minutes.

Prepare the sauce.
Melt the butter in a pot on low heat; add the crème fraîche, saffron and the orange juice. Mix and remove from heat. Decorate with chervil, top with the sauce and serve the flans warm (in the ramekins or removed form the mould).

Buttered Asparagus

Preparation : 10 mins
Cooking : 15 mins max

Simple !

An original and simple accompaniment, very quick!

Peel the asparagus and chop diagonally in small round slices, keeping the spears.

Melt the butter in a pan and brown the chopped asparagus stalks. Add the points of the asparagus.

Cooking : leave to cook for 10 to 15mins on low heat.
(The edges of the slices should not be too dark).

Sprinkle with sesame seeds before removing from the heat. Serve immediately.

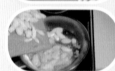

Asparagus with Ham and Parmesan

- salt/pepper
- parsley
- 4 tbsp grated parmesan
- 4 slices of uncooked ham
- 7–8 fine asparagus per person

Préparation : 10 mins
Cooking : 15 mins + 3 mins

A hot entree really refined and extremely easy.

Peel the asparagus and cook them whole in a stock made up of boiling water filled with the peelings for 20 minutes (increase the cooking time if the asparagus are really thick).
Place them lengthways in an oven-proof dish and interweave with some ham slices.
Sprinkle over with grated parmesan, some parmesan shavings and chopped parsley.
Place the dish for a **few minutes under the grill in the oven,** serve immediately.

37

Leeks

PREPARATION

1 Peel...

2 Wash...

3 Chop...

1

remove the end with the roots, cut the darkest leaves. Slit the leek from the white part until the end of the leaves.

2

wash under a strong jet of running water and open the leaves to ensure that all dirt and sand is removed.

3

in fine round slices to prepare leek fondue. In two or four pieces to make a soup. Leeks can also be cut lengthways in 'juliennes'.

38

THE LEEK HELPS ELIMINATION!

Fibres	water	proteins	carbohydrates	fats
2,7 g	91,5 g	1,2 g	3,9 g	0,2 g

Average nutritional composition of cooked leeks (for 100g)

ORIGINS AND PRODUCTION

Its origins are not fully known. It is thought that they come from the heart of the Mediterranean or from Asia.

However it has been known for a long time, as we say that the roman emperor Nero ate it regularly.

Some have suggested that it was the Romans who introduced the leek into Britain and Wales, who subsequently adopted the vegetable as their own.

In Britain it is grown in South West England and Wales.

It is picked principally from **September to March** but it can be found all year round depending on the regional production and imports.

NUTRITIONAL QUALITIES

Leeks contain a lot of water, few proteins, fats and carbohydrates. Therefore it is low in calories (21kcal/100g).

Carbohydrates and fibres are found in differing concentrations from the 'white' or the 'green' of the leek, which varies the flavours and textures.

The same can be said for the vitamins which are more concentrated in the green part.

HEALTH BENEFITS

It is important to eat all of the leek because of the difference in the nutritional composition between the 'white' and 'green' parts.

Leeks contain a particular carbohydrate which gives a diuretic effect by reinforcing the potassium/ sodium increase.

Information from the service of nutrition at the Institut Pasteur in Lille.

September to March

CHOOSING AND PRESERVING LEEKS

Choose leeks that are fresh and have a dark green colour.

It is necessary to cut the leave ends and to keep in the fridge. In this case the leeks will keep for 4 to 5 days.

It is possible to freeze leeks after blanching them, drain and leave in a freezer bag.

Leek Tagliatelle

Preparation : 10 mins
Cooking : 15 mins

Ingredients

- tagliatelle for 4 people
- 3 small leeks
- 100g grated parmesan
- 250g diced streaky bacon
- 250g button mushrooms
- salt/pepper
- 100g low fat crème fraîche
- knob of butter (optional)

Peel and carefully wash the leeks and **cut them in fine round slices.**

Brown the diced streaky bacon in a heavy-based deep pan. They can be browned with some butter (optional).

After 2 or 3 minutes, add the sliced leeks, mix and leave to cook for 5 to 7 minutes, mixing occasionally. Meanwhile, remove the mushroom stalks and **wash them quickly under cold water.** Slice them and add to the leeks. Add pepper.

Mix and leave to cook for 3 minutes. Add 2 tbsp of crème fraîche, mix. Cover and leave to cook for another 3 minutes.

Cook the pasta in salty water and drain. **Add 1 tbsp crème fraîche to the sauce, removed from heat,** and add 2 tbsp of grated parmesan. Mix well. Serve the taglietelle around a centre of sauce, sprinkle with some grated parmesan.

Leek Quiche

Preparation : 15 mins
Cooking : 20 mins

- 1 roll of ready made puff pastry
- chives
- 6 eggs
- 200g diced streaky bacon (smoked)
- Salt/pepper
- 1 glass of milk (or single cream)
- 3 leeks
- 100g grated gruyere
- 1/2 onion

After making a **LEEK FONDUE,** brown the diced streaky baco **(smoked)** in the same pan (after removing the leeks and reserving in separate plate). **Finely chop the chives.**

Whisk the eggs, add a pinch of salt (remember the bacon is already salty!). **Unroll the puff pastry** into a deep sided pastry tin. **Spread the leek fondue** on to the puff pastry. **Follow by the bacon** on top of the leeks **and then the chives. Add the egg mixture,** cover with grated gruye-re. Bake in the middle of the oven. 175°C – 30mins. Keep an eye on the baking, the quiche should rise after 15 to 20 minutes of cooking, and should turn a golden brown. If it browns too quickly it will not rise, adjust the oven temperature by reducing the heat.

Le Philosophe

Preparation : 20 mins
Cooking : 20 mins

Ingredients

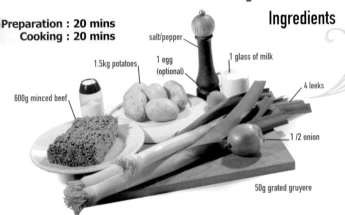

- 1.5kg potatoes
- salt/pepper
- 1 egg (optional)
- 1 glass of milk
- 600g minced beef
- 4 leeks
- 1/2 onion
- 50g grated gruyere

Prepare a **LEEK FONDUE**. Prepare a **POTATO PUREE** (to which you can add a whisked egg) **with 1.5kg of potatoes** (see the potato page).

Add some oil to a pan and **brown the onion**, finely chopped. When the onion becomes transparent, remove into a bowl.

Brown the **mince meat** in the same pan. When the mince is just cooked (3mins), **add** the **onion**. Season with salt and pepper. Next, fill the base of an oven-proof dish with the meat. **Cover with a layer of leek fondue.** Follow by a layer of the potato puree. Sprinkle with some grated gruyere. Bake in the middle of the oven, 200°C – 20mins.

> **Tip:** this recipe can be prepared a day in advance and kept in the refrigerator, and baked just before serving.

Leek Fondue

Melt 20g of butter in a large pan on low heat. Add little by little the **finely sliced leek** (preferable the lighter part of the leek). Season with salt and pepper. Mix until the leeks become slightly transparent.

Leave for about 10 minutes on a very low heat while stirring continuously.
The leeks should not brown.

Leek whites with White Wine

Place the leek fondue in a deep sided dish.
Add chunks of the white part of the leek, some thyme and some garlic. Pour over some white wine and vegetable stock.
Bake in the oven, in the middle, 200°C – 30mins.

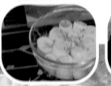

Cauliflower

PREPARATION

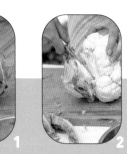
1

2

3

4

1 Remove
   leaves...
2 Cut the
   stalk...
3 Separate into
   florets...
4 Soak in
cold water...

soak in 1L of cold
water mixed with a
glass of vinegar.

CAULIFLOWER
and broccoli

Fibres	calcium	proteins	carbohydrates	vitamin C	fats
2,4 g	20 mg	2,4 g	2,3 g	50 mg	0,3 g

Average nutritional composition of cauliflower (for 100g)

ORIGINS AND PRODUCTION

Cauliflowers come from the Near East where they have been cultivated for more than 2000 years.

Greeks and Romans consumed large quantities in ancient times.

It's thanks to the Italians that the cauliflower arrived in France (some people say that it was the mafia who brought it…) whatever the truth, Louis XIV and Louis XV contributed greatly to its culinary use.

The largest producers of cauliflower are India and China.

Cauliflowers are mainly grown in England and there are more than 20 varieties which can be harvested all year round. However the largest consumption is between December and April.

NUTRITIONAL QUALITIES

Cauliflowers are low in calories (21kcal/100g). It contains little proteins (even if the level of proteins is higher than in other vegetables), fats and carbohydrates.

The concentration of vitamin C and B9 (folic acid), and fibres is high.

HEALTH BENEFITS

The principle benefit of eating cauliflowers is its concentration of vitamin C, especially when it is eaten raw. This vitamin is an antioxidant and plays a role in the protection against heart disease and some cancers.

The fibres present help regulate intestinal transit.

Information from the service of nutrition at the Institut Pasteur in Lille.

CHOOSING AND PRESERVING CAULIFLOWERS

December to April

The cauliflower should be chosen white and firm. The leaves should be green.
The preservation can last up to two or three days in the refrigerator, especially if its been washed, cut in small florets and kept in an airtight container.

Raw Grated Cauliflower

Broccoli sauteed with Almonds

Preparation : 10 mins
Cooking : 5 mins

Ingredients

- 1 small white cauliflower
- salt/pepper
- 2tbsp mayonnaise
- lemon juice
- 100g crushed nuts

- 2tbsp wine vinegar
- 1tsp coriander seeds
- 3tbsp olive oil
- 1tsp grilled sesame seeds
- 500g fresh broccoli
- salt/pepper
- 2tbsp flaked almonds
- 1 garlic clove minced

Separate the cauliflower into small florets. Grate **and pour over the lemon juice.** Season with salt and pepper. Leave to chill **for 15 minutes.**

Crush the nuts (by putting them in a grater for example). **Mix** the cauliflower, the nuts, and the mayonnaise.
Pour into the glasses and garnish with lemon and a little floret of cooked broccoli, for example.

Healthy Tip: you can mix 1/2 bowl of mayonnaise and 1/2 bowl of half-fat fromage frais.

Separate the broccoli into small bunches. **Crush the coriander seeds** (using a rolling pin).

Heat the oil in a large pan, **toast the coriander and almonds** on low heat (1 minute).

Add crushed garlic and the **broccoli.** Saute for about 4 minutes. Remove the pan from the heat and **add the vinegar to deglaze the pan. Stir** well and **add the sesame seeds** just before serving.

Cauliflower  Gratin

Preparation : 20 mins
Cooking : 15 mins + 10 mins

Ingredients

- 300ml milk
- salt/pepper
- 4 potatoes
- 100g grated gruyere
- 250ml low fat single cream
- Ham
- 1 cauliflower
- 2tbsp flour
- 2tbsp butter (for the béchamel)

Cook the cauliflower separated into small chunks and the chopped potatoes together in salted water, 15mins.

Make a béchamel sauce (see pages 'Pumpkin Soufflé'). **Drain, place** the potatoes in an oven-proof dish and the cauliflower in the centre. **Garnish with slices of ham.**

Pour over the béchamel sauce or the cream. **Sprinkle over the grated gruyere.**

Bake in a heated oven (200°C) for 10mins until the gruyere turns golden.

Steamed 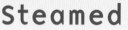 Broccoli — Simple !

Preparation : 5 mins
Cooking : 4 mins

Separate the broccoli into small florets. Cut the stalks when too long. Place in a pot with 2cm of salted water and cover.
Leave to cook 4mins.
(Even better: steam cook if you have a steamer.)
Serve as a side dish to meat or fish or as tapas with a sauce of fromage frais with herbs.

Warm Cauliflower Salad

Boil the florets of 1/2 cauliflower in **salted water**, 10mins.
Place quickly under cold water (the cauliflower should be 'al dente').
Season with a slightly lemony vinaigrette and sprinkle over some chives.

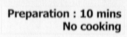

Crunchy raw Cauliflower

Preparation : 10 mins
No cooking

Separate the cauliflower into small bunches. So that they stay white, **plunge the florets of cauliflower in 1L of cold water mixed with 1 glass of vinegar** for 10mins.
Prepare the cocktail sauce and chives.
Drain the cauliflower and dry on absorbent paper.
Present the cauliflower and the sauces in small dishes. To be eaten with fingers.

Chive Sauce: mix 2tbsp of chopped chives with 3tbsp of crème fraîche (or fresh goats cheese). **Add pepper – mix.**

Light Cocktail Sauce: Mix 1/2 tsp of mustard with 3 tbsp fromage blanc and 2 tbsp ketchup. **Add** 1/2 tsp of curry powder. **Mix.**

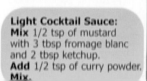

Carrots

PREPARATION

1 Peel...

2 Trim...

3 Round slices
or chunks...

4 Juliennes...

peel the carrots with a
vegetable peeler.

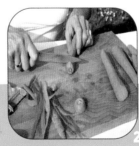

remove the top part of
the carrot.

cut the
carrots into round slices.

chop the
carrots lengthways
into juliennes

...res	carotenes	proteins	Carbohydrates	vitamin C	fats
..g	10 000 µg	0,8 g	6,7 g	7 mg	0,3 g

**Average nutritional composition
of carrots (for 100g)**

ORIGINS AND PRODUCTION

Carrots are originally from Asia Minor, perhaps Afghanistan where it was harvested in its wild state and didn't have the colour we are familiar with.

The first carrots to be cultivated in Europe were yellow or purple. It was in Holland, from the 1600s, that we found carrots more orange in colour. The vegetable as we know it today could be found from the 19th century.

China produces more than 30% of the world's production.

There are many varieties of carrots and they can be found in mostly England but also other areas of Britain.

It can be found in supermarkets all year long.

NUTRITIONAL QUALITIES

Carrots are part of the group of vegetables which can be eaten just as well raw as cooked.
Of course, during its raw state it contains the most vitamins.
Even if it contains more calories than most other vegetables thanks to its level of sugar, it calorie level still remains low. (31kcal/100g).
Carrots have two major nutritional benefits: its level of fibres and caroetenes, especially betacarotene, which gives it the orange colour (the latter is lower in yellow carrots).

HEALTH BENEFITS

Eating 100g of carrots give half of the bodys need for Vitamin A. This vitamin, found in carotenes, helps growth, eyesight and works against the beginning of cancer.

The richness of fibres helps the regulate intestinal transit, whether it be constipation or diarrhoea. It also helps the elimination of cholesterol.

Its glyceamic index is much lower than normally believed, making it ideal for all diets.

Information from the service of nutrition at the Institut Pasteur in Lille.

CHOOSING AND PRESERVING CARROTS

All year round

Fresh carrots should be firm and lustrous. Its leaves should be green and fresh. If the carrots were bought with leaves it is better to cut them as soon as possible, to avoid the loss of moisture and softening of the vegetable.

Glazed Carrots with onions

Preparation : 5 mins
Cooking : 15 mins

- salt/pepper
- 8 medium carrots
- 4 spring onions (whites)
- 25g butter (+ little olive oil)
- 1 sprig thyme

Peel and chop the carrots in round pieces. Peel and cut **the onions** into large chunks (or in two if they are not too large). Melt the butter and a little olive oil in a pot on low heat, and brown the onions. Rapidly **add** the **carrots** and **thyme**, salt and pepper.

Leave to cook without covering and **mix lightly**, the onions should become slightly transparent. Half-way through cooking, you can add a **tbsp of sugar** to lightly brown. Pour in a little water, cover and leave on low heat for 10mins.

Baby Carrot Parcels

Ingredients

Preparation : 5 mins
Cooking : 20 mins

- 1 glass good white wine
- salt/pepper
- 4 carrots per person
- some sprigs of tarragon
- 25g butter (optional)
- aromatic herbs
- 1 small glass olive oil

Place 4 carrots per person in a sheet of aluminium foil.

Add the herbs and the salt and pepper. Lifts the edges of the aluminium paper.

Pour over the olive oil and the white wine or a knob of butter and white wine in the 4 parcels and seal the edges of the foil.

Bake in the oven for a minimum 20mins, more if the carrots are thicker.

If the carrots are very young and small, leave some of the greens and don't peel them. If they are large then peel them completely.

Carrot and Pesto Lasagne

Preparation : 20 mins
Cooking : 40 mins

Ingredients

- 750ml milk
- 160g single cream
- 50g butter
- 4 lightly whisked eggs
- 2tbsp pesto
- 1tsp crushed black pepper
- 750g peeled and grated carrots
- 150g grated cheese
- 60g flour
- lasagne sheets ready to use

Peel and grate the carrots. On low heat, **melt the butter** in a pot and **add the flour.** Mix until it browns and starts to bubble. Add **the milk** little by little, then **the cream** while constantly mixing, add pepper. Leave to cook for 5mins on medium heat, mix until thickens and remove from the heat. **Add 100g of cheese** and leave to cool slightly. **Add the eggs,** mix.

Reserve 1/3 of the sauce in a bowl for garnishing. **Add the pesto** and the **grated carrots** in the rest of the sauce, mix well.

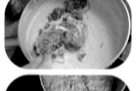

In a buttered lasagne dish, add 1/3 of the carrot sauce, alternate the **layers: sauce/lasagne** sheets finishing with a pasta sheet. **Pour over the bowl of reserved sauce** and cover with cheese. **Leave to rest for 15mins** to allow the lasagne sheets to soften.

Bake in the oven for 40mins at 160°C. Remove from the oven, cover and leave to rest for 15mins before serving: the gratin should be easier to cut. Serve with a green salad.

Grated Carrots

Simple !

Count 2 carrots per person. **Grate and season** with a simple vinaigrette, **add sliced shallots,** serve cold. For a more sophisticated seasoning **add orange blossom water** and the juice of 1 orange (reduce the amount of oil in the vinaigrette), or you can add **curry powder** and some **raisins.**

an essential cruditee

Carrot Puree

Ingredients :
3 potatoes
1 onion, salt/pepper
5 to 6 carrots
Crème fraîche
Cumin

Brown the sliced onions in a pot, **add** round slices of carrots. **Peel and cut** the potatoes in 4. Season with salt and pepper (you can add powdered cumin for a stronger taste). Add some water and cook for 15mins. Drain. Mash with a puree maker. Cook further for 5 to 10mins to reduce. Cover and leave to cook for 15mins. Add 1 tbsp of crème fraîche before serving.

Carrots and Grapefruit

Ingredients :
2 grapefruits
3 carrots
1tbsp of lemon juice
2 tbsp olive oil
Salt/pepper

Preparation: cut the grapefruit in two, scoop out the inside and cut the flesh into cubes. **Grate the carrots; mix with the cubes of grapefruit.** Pour over the lemon juice mixed with olive oil and salt and pepper. Check the seasoning and fill the grapefruits. **Decorate with some flat parsley and slices of boiled egg if desired.**

Turnips

PREPARATION

  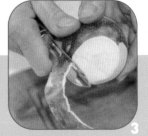 

1 Cut
   the root...
2 Trim
   the top...
3 Peel...
4 Chop...

FACTS ABOUT
TURNIPS

Fibres	calcium	proteins	carbohydrates	vitamin C	fats
2,1 g	33 mg	0,8 g	2,9 g	11 mg	0,1 g

**Average nutritional composition
of turnips (for 100g)**

ORIGINS AND PRODUCTION

Turnips are originally from Europe but it has also been cultivated in India for thousands of years.

This root vegetable used to be one of the most eaten vegetables on a daily basis. This is not true today as it has been replaced by potatoes.

The most common type is white with a purple head but completely white turnips can also be found as well as yellow-orange.

In full season turnips are harvested in the UK from **October to June.**

NUTRITIONAL QUALITIES

Turnips are low in protein, fats and sugars but contain a lot of water. It is therefore low in calories (15kcal).
It has a higher level of fibres at 2%.
Turnips contain many salt minerals, it is rich in potassium.

HEALTH BENEFITS

Turnips are important as part of a healthy and balanced diet, it possesses non-nutritional compounds which produce a preventative action against certain cancers which depend on oestrogen like breast cancer.

Its potassium level is useful for regulating arterial blood pressure, like all vegetables.

Information from the service of nutrition at the Institut Pasteur in Lille.

October to June

CHOOSING AND PRESERVING TURNIPS

A fresh turnip is firm, smooth and heavy. It is preferable to choose it young to avoid it being spongy or fibrous.
It should be kept in a cool, dark place, or eventually in the refrigerator, not more than a week for young turnips,
2 weeks for others.

Glazed Turnips and Fresh Duck Fillet

Preparation : 20 mins
Cooking : 30 mins

Ingredients

salt/pepper
2tbsp sugar
20g butter
700g small turnips
parsley
1 duck fillet

Peel and trim the base and leaves of the turnip. **Very small turnips can be cooked whole without peeling** (remove the base with the leaves). Chop into cubes. Melt the butter in a pot or a deep sided pan.

Mix, add salt and pepper. When the turnips become slightly transparent, add the sugar and mix. Leave to cook covered for 10 to 15mins.

Mix and deglaze by adding 3tbsp of water. Continue to cook for a few more minutes.
Sprinkle with chopped parsley.
Cook the fillet of duck 10mins skin side in a pan (without any oil and taking care to cut the skin) + 3mins on the flesh side.
Place the duck fillets in each plate with a portion of the glazed turnips.

Stuffed Turnips

Preparation : 20 mins
Cooking : 15 mins + 50 mins

2 turnips per person
salt/pepper
350g minced meat
1 onion
some sprigs parsley

Remove the root (cutting so that the turnip can sit easily) and **the leaves of the turnip.**
Wash them with cold water (with the help of a brush if they are dirty), **don't peel them.** Cook the turnips in salted boiling water for 15mins.

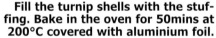

Drain them and place on absorbent paper after cooking. **Scoop out the flesh and keep the flesh in a bowl.** Mix in a food processor. Mix with the minced meat, finely chopped parsley, and chopped onion. Add salt and pepper.

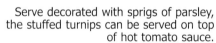

Fill the turnip shells with the stuffing. Bake in the oven for 50mins at 200°C covered with aluminium foil.

Serve decorated with sprigs of parsley, the stuffed turnips can be served on top of hot tomato sauce.

Tarte Tatin of Turnip confit with smoked Duck Fillet

Preparation : 25 mins
Cooking : 5 mins + 25 mins

Baby Turnip Salad

- 300ml white wine
- 2tbsp balsamic vinegar
- salt/pepper
- 200g smoked duck fillet fine slices
- 50g powdered sugar
- 1 roll puff pastry
- 1.2kg turnips
- 2tbsp orange juice
- 40g butter

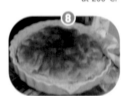

Add the turnips to the syrup, then leave to cook partly covered stirring frequently until they are tender and covered with a layer of syrup (about 10mins).

Preparation : 10 mins /one night in the refrigerator

- balsamic vinegar
- olive oil
- salt/pepper
- 2 turnips per person

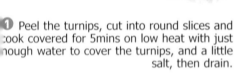

① Peel the turnips, cut into round slices and cook covered for 5mins on low heat with just enough water to cover the turnips, and a little salt, then drain.

② **In a pot, reduce the wine to half its volume (on high heat).** Caramelise the sugar with a drop of water in a pan, add a knob of butter when the sugar has dissolved.

③ **Away from the heat. Add the vinegar and orange juice,** mix vigorously.

④ Place on the heat; add the wine, 50g of butter, salt and pepper.

Cover the base of the tart tin with greaseproof paper. **Layer the turnips.**

Place over the puff pastry pricked with a fork and cover the edges with the pastry. Bake for 25mins at 200°C.

Cut the baby turnips into fine 2mm slices, washed but not peeled.

In a salad bowl add 150ml olive oil mixed with 1/4 garlic clove finely chopped and 1tbsp of balsamic vinegar or red wine vinegar, salt and pepper.

Mix the seasoning with the turnips and leave to marinate overnight in the refrigerator covered with cling film.

A starter or an aperitif.

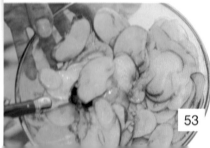

Leave to cook for 5mins, and then **turn out into a plate.** Decorate with the smoked duck.

Cucumbers

PREPARATION

1 Peel...

2 Chop...

3 Salt...

1

with a potato peeler, or simply with a knife to guard some of the skin (that has been washed).

2

in fine round slices, sticks or chunks, depending on the recipe you are making.

3

to remove some of the water, place the slices of cucumber in a salad bowl and sprinkle over 1tbsp of sea salt and leave for 10 mins. Next, place on some absorbent paper before seasoning.

CUCUMBERS, HYDRATING CHAMPION!

| fibres 0,8 g | calcium 19 mg | proteins 0,7 g | carbohydrates 2 g | vitamine C 5 mg | lipides 0,1 g |

Average nutritional composition of cucumbers (for 100g)

ORIGINS AND PRODUCTION

Cucumbers originally come from Asia. It seems that they were cultivated in China 5000 years ago.

In ancient times, the Greeks and Romans consumed cucumbers regularly.

Charlemagne introduced it to his empire but it wasn't until the 17th century that it was used widely in France and it was two centuries later that it was first cultivated in 19th century England.

Nowadays, China is responsible for more than 60% of the world's production.

In Britain production peaks from **July to September.**

NUTRITIONAL QUALITIES

Cucumbers are rich in water (96%), poor in fats, carbohydrates and proteins. They are therefore low in calories (11kcal/100g).

Numerous minerals, trace elements and vitamins are present in cucumbers but in low quantities.

HEALTH BENEFITS

The cucumber is a vegetable which is important in a balanced and varied diet.

Thanks to its high potassium/sodium levels, the cucumber is a diuretic vegetable.

It also contributes to the control of arterial pressure.

Information from the service of nutrition at the Institut Pasteur in Lille.

CHOOSING AND PRESERVING CUCUMBERS

July to September

Cucumbers should be chosen when they are lustrous, firm and green.

They can be stored easily in the vegetable compartment in the refrigerator. If a cucumber has been sliced it is better to protect it by covering with some cling film.

Do not keep cucumbers at room temperature as they will dry very quickly and will lose their crunchy texture.

Mediterranean Salad

Ingredients

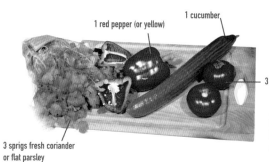

1 red pepper (or yellow)

1 cucumber

3 tomatoes

Juice of 1/2 lemon (or vinegar)
2tbsp olive oil
salt

3 sprigs fresh coriander or flat parsley

Mix equal quantities of **red peppers, tomatoes,** and **cucumber** cut into small cubes.

Add the coriander leaves cut into small pieces.

Pour over the lemon juice and the **olive oil.**

Season with salt.

Serve chilled.

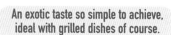

An exotic taste so simple to achieve, ideal with grilled dishes of course.

Cucumber Canapés

2 cucumbers

salt/pepper

prawns or crab (shelled)

prawn salad

crab salad

tzatziki

Chop the cucumbers in large chunks of about 4cm, without peeling.
Remove the flesh of each piece with a small spoon without breaking the base.

Fill each piece of cucumber with the **readymade salad,** the tzatziki, tuna mayonnaise, crab salad etc

Decorate however you like.

Tartare of Salmon with Cucumber

Preparation : 5 mins
No cooking

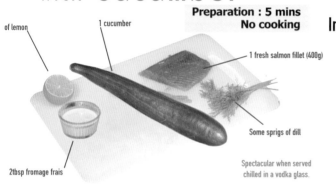

- of lemon
- 1 cucumber
- 1 fresh salmon fillet (400g)
- Some sprigs of dill
- 2tbsp fromage frais

Spectacular when served chilled in a vodka glass.

Ingredients

Cut the raw salmon and **the peeled cucumber** into small cubes (avoid using a food processor as the salmon will be reduced to a puree).

Finely chop the dill and mix all three ingredients. **Pour over the lemon juice** and add in the fromage frais.

Divide into cocktail glasses and sprinkle over some dill. Chill in the refrigerator for **at least 30mins and serve cold.**

Serving suggestion as cocktail or starter.

Cream of Cucumber with Peppers

Preparation : 10 mins
Cooking : 30 mins

- 2 green peppers
- 1 egg yolk
- 2 small cucumbers
- 100g low fat crème fraîche
- 1tbsp butter
- nutmeg
- 3 onions
- 1 bunch of flat parsley
- 2 stock cubes dissolved in 1.5L of hot water
- 3 ground cloves

Chop the onions and brown in a little butter or oil.

Add the pepper cut into fine slices, as well as the cucumber cut into fine sticks, taking care beforehand to peel them and leave them to salt for 10 mins to lose a little water and then wipe with absorbent paper.

Pour in the meat stock water. Season with salt, pepper, nutmeg and the ground clove powder. Bring the mixture to boil and leave to **cook gently for about 30mins.**

Mix in a food blender and bring back to the boil.

Blend in the egg yolk and the crème fraîche. Before serving, decorate with some chopped parsley.

Cucumber Salad

Basic!

Peel and cut the cucumber into round slices. Sprinkle over one tbsp of sea salt and leave **15mins** in the refrigerator so that it loses a little water.

Drain and season to taste.

A simple and rapid accompaniment!

Celeriac

PREPARATION

1 Quarter...

2 Peel...

3 Chop...

1 cut the celeriac in half
and remove the large roots and thick skin with a knife.

2

3 cut the celeriac in small
cubes or larger pieces if
you want to grate it.

ibres	calcium	proteins	carbohydrates	Sodium	fats
5 g	43 mg	1,5 g	2,4 g	100 mg	0,3 g

Average nutritional composition of celeriac (for 100g)

ORIGINS AND PRODUCTION

The celeriac as we know it today is a wild plant eaten in Europe and Asia for a long time. During the renaissance gardeners produced plants which had a more delicate taste.

The harvest season of celeriac is during autumn, in October in general before the frost. Certain varieties can be harvested in summer.

France is the leading producer of celeriac in Europe. In Britain is harvested from **mid-September to the end of April.**

NUTRITIONAL QUALITIES

Celeriac is low in calories (18kcal/100g) because it is low in carbohydrates, fats and proteins.

This root vegetable is richer in sodium than other vegetables and has higher levels of potassium and calcium. It contains a high quantity of fibres.

HEALTH BENEFITS

Being rich in potassium, the celeriac has a positive effect on the cardiac system.

This vegetable is not recommended in low sodium diets because of its high level of sodium.

The presence of fibres helps regulate intestinal transit by fighting against constipation.

Information from the service of nutrition at the Institut Pasteur in Lille.

CHOOSING AND PRESERVING CELERIAC

September to April

A fresh celeriac is heavy and firm. It should not sound hollow when it is tapped. It can be conserved unpeeled in the refrigerator in the vegetable compartment for a week.

Celeriac Puree

Preparation : 15 mins
Cooking : 25 mins

2tbsp low fat crème fraîche
1 celeriac (less than 1kg)
4 potatoes
Grated gruyere
1tbsp butter (optional)
1 egg yolk
Grated nutmeg

Tips for peeling celeriac: cut firstly in half with a large knife. **Peel the celeriac** and chop into small cubes. Repeat these steps with the potatoes.

Cook both vegetables together for 20mins in a pot with salted water adding a little grated nutmeg. **Drain and mash** the potatoes and the celeriac. **Add the egg yolk**, the butter and the crème fraîche.

Pour into a oven-proof dish. Sprinkle over the grated gruyere and add some knobs of butter (optional).

Bake under the grill for 5 minutes.

NB: you can cook double the quantity of potatoes/celeriac to prepare the cream of celeriac and the celeriac puree at the same time.

Cream of celeriac with Roquefort

Ingredients

Preparation : 15 mins
Cuisson : 20 mins
(10 mn in pressure cooker)

salt/pepper
100g Roquefort
100 ml low fat single cream
1 head of celeriac (less than 1kg)
1 stock cube in 1.5L of water
A handful of crushed nuts
2 or 3 potatoes

Peel the celeriac and the potatoes. **Cut the vegetables in medium sized cubes.** Place the vegetables in a pressure-cooker covered with water.

Lightly salt (because of the Roquefort), season with pepper and add the stock cube. Close the pressure-cooker **and leave to cook for 10 minutes** from the minute the valve sounds (or 20 minutes using a traditional pot).

Once the cooking is over **blend the mixture without draining and add the cream** along with the Roquefort and the nuts. Taste and adjust the seasoning if necessary.
The amount of water depends on the thickness of the cream you want to achieve.
If you do not have any potatoes add 3 carrots: this simply changes the colour of the mixture.

NB: this freezes well.

Celeriac Cakes

Preparation : 20 mins
Cooking : 30 mins

100ml low fat crème fraîche

salt/pepper

40g cornflour

2 eggs

Grated nutmeg

1kg celeriac

Peel the celeriac, cut it into small pieces, cook for 20mins in boiling salted water. Drain in a sieve for a few minutes. **Mash into a puree and mix** with the corn flour, whisked eggs, the crème fraîche and seasoning.

Make small round cakes using floured hands and place them on a buttered oven-proof dish.

Bake for 30mins on medium heat in the oven. These cakes can be served as a side dish to meat.

Celeriac Remoulade

Ingredients

celeriac

salt/pepper

1 bowl
1/2 mayonnaise
1/2 low-fat crème fraîche

lemon

Peel the celeriac and **chop** in large chunks. Grate the celeriac with a food processor. **Pour** over a **little lemon juice.**

Mix the grated celeriac with the mayonnaise and **the low fat crème fraîche** (or fromage frais with 20% fat).

Chill in the fridge.

Buttered Celeriac

Cooking : 20 mins

Peel and chop the celeriac into small cubes.

Cook for 15mins in a pot with salted boiling water. **Drain, melt 50g of butter** in a casserole dish and brown the cubes of celeriac for 5mins in the butter.

Sprinkle over the chopped parsley. Serve immediately.

Green beans

PREPARATION

1 Trim...

2 Cook...

GREEN BEANS, GREAT PROTECTORS

Information from the service of nutrition at the Institut Pasteur in Lille.

FACTS ABOUT
GREEN BEANS

iron	fibres	calcium	Proteins	carbohydrates	vitamin C	fats
1,2 mg	**3 g**	40 mg	1,8 g	3,9 g	**10 mg**	0,2 g

**Average nutritional composition
of green beans (for 100g)**

NUTRITIONAL QUALITIES

Green beans are low in calories (24kcal/100g) because it is low in carbohydrates, fats and rich in water. The amount of proteins is slightly higher than in other vegetables because it is a legume.

Its concentration of fibres, calcium, iron, provitamin A, vitamin B and vitamin C (the same quantity when cooked as when raw) is high.

ORIGINS AND PRODUCTION

Green beans originate from South America where its seeds have been consumed dried more than 8000 years ago.

They arrived in Europe in the 16th century.

It was in the 18th century when the Italians were the first to eat fresh green beans in the form of vege-tables.

The harvest season in Britain is from **June to September.**

HEALTH BENEFITS

It is the epitome of weight loss foods. However, eating too much can leave you weary: one should vary the foods and vegetables that are eaten.

Provitamin A and vitamin C have antioxidant effects and work to protect against certain cancers and fight against cardiovascular diseases.

Vitamin B9 plays a protective role against the malformation of the neural tube of the foetus.

Iron allows the body to fight against anaemia and infections.

CHOOSING AND PRESERVING GREEN BEANS

June to September

When buying fresh green beans they should be firm and should snap when you bend them.
It is possible to keep green beans in the refrigerator for 3 to 4 day and they can also be frozen.

Salade Niçoise

Preparation : 10 mins
Cooking : 10 mins

salt/pepper
1 white onion
250g rocket
2 small peppers
anchovies
1 bunch radish
2 tomatoes
2 boiled eggs
Some basil leaves
Handful of black olives (petites niçoises)
1 tin of tuna in brine
250g cooked green beens

Cook 250g of green beans in a pot of salted boiling water for 10mins, drain. Boil two eggs till hard. Wash the tomatoes and cut into round slices. Peel and chop the onion. trim and wash the radishes. Place the rocket in the base of a salad bowl.

Add the chopped onion, sliced radishes, tomatoes, sliced peppers, and the green beans. Crumble in the tuna. Add the black olives, spread around the boiled eggs chopped into four. Season with olive oil, pepper and salt. Decorate with some fresh basil and some anchovies.

Green Beans à la Tomate

Ingredients

Preparation : 15 mins
Cooking : 10 mins

salt/pepper
2tbsp wine vinegar
2tbsp olive oil
1 chopped onion
2tbsp powdered sugar
400g tomatoes
20 crushed black olives
Some chopped basil leaves
500g green beans
2 garlic cloves crushed

Trim the green beans and cut into two. **Cook for 3mins** in boiling salted water. Refresh them under cold water. Brown the onions for 3mins in some oil. **Add the sugar and garlic**. Mix. Leave to caramelise.

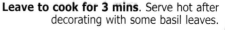

Add the vinegar. Mix. Leave to cook for 3 mins.

Add the olives and basil.
Add the tomatoes cut into small pieces. Leave to reduce for a few minutes. **Add the green beans**. Season with salt and pepper.

Leave to cook for 3 mins. Serve hot after decorating with some basil leaves.

Green Beans
with Tagliatelle

Preparation : 20 mins
Cooking : 15 mins

Ingredients

- tagliatelle
- salt/pepper
- 75g grated cheese
- 150g low fat single cream
- 250g ham slices (very fine)
- 1 garlic clove
- 30g butter
- 150g green beans

Wash the green beans, chop them into pieces and cook them uncovered in boiling salted water till done (7 to 10 mins depending on thickness).

Drain and cook them in the butter with the crushed garlic, season. **Add the cream and slices of ham.**

Keep everything hot. Meanwhile, boil a large volume of water to cook the tagliatelle, add a little oil to prevent them sticking to each other, salt, remove the pasta.

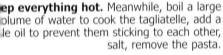

Drain the pasta; add the grated cheese and the prepared green bean sauce. Mix and serve immediately. Decorate with some parmesan shavings.

Buttered
Mangetout

Preparation : 10 mins
Cooking : 20 mins

Ingredients :
700g mangetout
(large flat green beans)
1 large onion
Olive oil
Chopped parsley
Salt/pepper

Trip and chop the mangetout into small pieces. Boil them for 15mins in salted water. In a pot brown 1/4 of the large onion in 1 tbsp of oil. Add the mangetout. **Leave them to cook for a few minutes. Add a knob of butter and the chopped parsley.** Lightly pepper. Serve immediately.

Green Bean
Bundles

Ingredients for 1 bundle:
1 slice of bacon, 15 cooked green beans.

Cook 500g of green beans in 1 litre of salted boiling water, 5mins.

Melt the bacon slices in a pan to melt the fat, leave them on some absorbent paper.

Cook and drain the green beans. **Divide about 15 green beans for each bundle and roll with a slice of bacon.**

Cook for **15 to 20 mins** in a hot oven and serve with meat.

NB: the bundles can be cooked in the same dish as the meat (with roast for example).

Mushrooms

Button, Oyster and Chanterelles

PREPARATION

1 Clean...

2 Chop...

3 Season with lemon...

use absorbent paper or a brush to remove any traces of earth under the mushrooms.

Information from the service of nutrition at the Institut Pasteur in Lille.

FACTS ABOUT
MUSHROOMS

...bres	vitamin B2	vitamin B3	vitamin B5	Proteins	carbohydrates	potassium	lipides
...5 g	0,45 mg	4 mg	2,2 mg	2,1 g	0,5 g	372 mg	0,5 g

**Average nutritional composition of raw
button mushrooms (for 100 g)**

ORIGINS AND PRODUCTION

Multiple varieties of mushrooms grow wild, but of course not all types are edible.

We only find a limited amount of cultivated varieties: button mushrooms (the most familiar), chanterelles, oyster, porcini, portobello…each has a distinctive texture and flavour.

Our prehistoric ancestors already ate wild mushrooms, but it was the gardener of Louis XIV and a French agriculturist in the 18th century who improved the cultivating techniques.

In France, the leading producer of mushrooms in Europe, button mushrooms are harvested all year long.

NUTRITIONAL QUALITIES

Mushrooms are low in fat and carbohydrates. They contains slightly more proteins than the majority of vegetables but contrary to popular belief, they are not a replacement for meat. They are rich in water. The calories found in them are therefore low (15kcal/100g).
The concentration of potassium is quite high.
It contains an important amount of vitamins B2, B3 and B5.
Mushrooms are a good source of iodine.

HEALTH BENEFITS

Potassium helps the cardiovascular system.

The vitamins B2 and B3 are necessary for growth. They both play a role in the metabolism of proteins. Vitamin B2 also plays a role in the breaking down of carbohydrates and fats.

Vitamin B5 helps to maintain healthy skin, hair and mucus membrane.

CHOOSING AND PRESERVING MUSHROOMS

Choose mushrooms that are smooth and unblemished.
The cap, firm, should be solid and attached to the stem. It is better if the underside of the cap is not seen.
If this is not the case, the underside should be light in colour.

Stuffed Mushrooms

Preparation : 10 mins
Cooking : 15 mins

- 250g large button mushrooms
- salt/pepper
- 150g ham chopped
- 100g gorgonzola
- 1/2 onion chopped

Remove the mushrooms stalks. Wash the mushrooms.

Scrape out the inside of the cap and keep the flesh for the garniture. Brown the chopped onions, add the finely sliced stalks.

Away from the heat add the ham chopped into small cubes.

Stuff the cap of each mushroom with this mixture and **cover with the gorgonzola.**

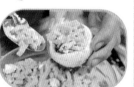

Bake for 10 to 15mins in a very hot oven. Serve immediately.

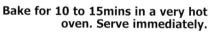

Mushroom Fricassee in an Omelette

Ingredients

Preparation : 10 mins
Cooking : 5-6 mins

- 300g oyster mushrooms
- Sprigs of parsley
- 20g butter
- Salt/pepper
- 300g chanterelles
- 300g button mushrooms
- 2 garlic cloves
- 2tbsp olive oil
- 8 eggs for the omel...

Remove the sandy stems of the button mushrooms. Chop them into 4 if they are large. **Clean the oyster mushrooms and the chanterelles** with a brush to delicately remove the sand. Do not wash them, cut them in large chunks.

Peel the garlic and remove the germ. Chop into small pieces. Mince the parsely. Pour some oil into a pan. **Brown the mushroom medley and mix regularly.** If they 'release' some water remove it. Season with salt, pepper, leave to cook for 5 mins.

Add garlic and leave to cook for 3 more minutes. Just before removing from heat sprinkle over the parsley and keep the mushrooms hot (in the oven at 80°C).

Whisk the eggs for omelette, season with and pepper. Cook in a fold the omelet two while it is still m Add the mushro to the Leave to cook for and serve immedia
Cooki
5-6 m

Mushroom soup

Preparation : 15 mins
Cooking : 15 mins

- 500ml low fat single cream
- 1.5kg button mushrooms
- salt/pepper
- Some parsly sprigs
- 1 onion
- 2 chicken stock cubes in 1.5L water

Ingredients

Chop the onion.
Brown them in a pot.
Add the mushrooms, cleaned and cut into slices.
Add salt and pepper.
Mix with the stock.
Leave to cook covered for 15mins.
Smooth in a blender.
Add the cream.

Tip: brown some mushroom slices in a pan to decorate before serving, or sprinkle over some chopped parsley.

Greek-style Mushrooms

Preparation : 15 mins
Cooking : 25 mins

- 1/2 glass oil
- salt/pepper
- 1 glass white wine
- 500g button mushrooms
- 10 grelot onions
- Some thyme sprigs
- 2 bay leaves

Clean the mushrooms by dipping them briefly in some water mixed with vinegar. Wipe them. If they are very small leave them whole, if not quarter them. **Mix the oil, white wine, thyme and bay leaves in a large pot.** Heat gently. Add the peeled onions (cut them in half if they are too large). **Add the mushrooms.** Cook covered on low heat. **Cook for 25mins. Serve cold.** This dish can be kept for several days in the refrigerator (cover with cling film).

Mushrooms on Toast

Preparation : 10 mins
Cooking : 10 mins

- 500g button mushrooms
- Bread to be toasted
- Some low fat crème fraîche
- 250g diced streaky bacon
- Some branches of chives

Clean the mushrooms and slice them. **Brown the diced streaky bacon a little** in a pan without adding any fat.

During this time grill the bread in a toaster. Add the bacon to the mushrooms, lightly pepper.

Fold in some crème fraîche. Leave to cook for 5mins. Garnish the toast by decorating with some chives.

69

Fennel

PREPARATION

1 Remove the base...
2 Trim the leaves..
3 Halve...
4 Remove the core ...
5 Slice...

1   2   3   4   5

| calcium mg | fibres 3,3 g | vitamin B9 15 µg | proteins 1,1 g | carbohydrates 2,3 g | potassium 473 mg | fats 0,3 g |

Average nutritional composition of uncooked fennel (for 100g)

ORIGINS AND PRODUCTION

Fennel originally comes from the Mediterranean basin. The seeds can be used to flavour quick stocks but it is mostly the bulb that is used as a vegetable.

It seems that it was cultivated in the royal gardens in France in the 15th century but in Italy it held a privileged position more than in France.

It wasn't until during the 17th century that it was introduced to Britain from Italy.

Harvested all year round in Italy and in Spain, it is produced in Britain mostly during **June to October.**

NUTRITIONAL QUALITIES

Fennel is rich in water, low in carbohydrates, fats and proteins. It contains therefore few calories. (16kcal/100g)

It contains an important level of fibres, as well as potassium, and a little of folic acid (vitamin B9).

HEALTH BENEFITS

The potassium takes part in good cardiovascular function. Vitamin B9 helps to prevent the malformation of the neural tube (the nervous system and the spinal chord) of a foetus called Spina Bifida.

Information from the service of nutrition at the Institut Pasteur in Lille.

CHOOSING AND PRESERVING FENNEL

June to October

When it is fresh and of good quality, fennel is white and unblemished, smooth and firm.
The leaves should be green.
Fennel can be kept in the vegetable compartment in the refrigerator for up to a week.
To prevent its smell from escaping it can be kept in an airtight container.

Haddock Fillet on a bed of Fennel

Chicken with Fenne

Preparation : 10 mins
Cooking : 25 mins

2 large fennel bulbs

salt/pepper

1 large glass of white wine

1 knob of butter

1 fillet of fish (500g) (haddock or even fillets of red mullet)

chives

Cut the bulbs in two, remove the core and then cut into slices. Places at the base of an oven-proof dish. Season with salt and pepper.

Place the fillet of fish on the bed of fennel. Season with salt and pepper. **Pour the white wine on the base of the dish.** Add some knobs of butter on the fish and some branches of chives.

You can also sprinkle over the sprigs of fennel leaves before covering the dish with aluminium foil.

Bake in the oven at 200°C for 25mins. Remove the aluminium foil 5mins before the end of cooking.

Chicken with Fenne

Preparation : 15 mins
Cooking : 5 mins + 20 mins

Ingredients
for 4 pers.

salt/pepper

1tbsp olive oil

4 fennel bulbs

1tbsp pastis

4 chicken fillets

1 chicken stock cube dissolved in 250ml warm water

rosemary Provencal Herbs (op

Cut the fennel bulbs in not-too-fine slices. **Cook them in wate mix, drain.** (They should not be soft, but the edge a knife should be able to pierce it). You can also cook the fennel in a pan (5mins).

Cut the chicken fillets in fine strips. **Spread the base of a dish with fennel,** cover with the strips of chicken, then again with the fennel.

Mix the chicken stock, pastis and olive oil. Pour over the fennel and chicken.

Season with salt and pepper, sprinkle over some dill, rosemary or provencal herbs.

Bake for 20mins at gas mark 6 (180°C).

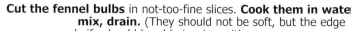

Tarte Tatin of Fennel with Blue Cheese

Preparation : 15 mins
Cooking : 5 mins + 30 mins

Ingredients

- 1tbsp olive oil
- 2tsp butter
- 1tbsp runny honey
- 1 ready made pastry
- 1 large fennel bulb or 2 small
- powdered sugar
- 1 slice of blue cheese
- Optional: oregano, crushed nuts

Chop the fennel. **Place it in a large pan** with the olive oil on high heat to brown them, then add the honey and lower the heat (5mins).

Cover the tart tin with cooking paper (aluminium foil). Pour the fennel on to the foil, add salt and pepper to taste, then cover with the blue cheese depending on how much you prefer. **Place the ready-made pastry** on top and carefully seal the edges.

Place in the oven for 30mins at 210°C (gas mark 7), check the cooking of the pastry before removing. Turn out into a serving plate of your choice and carefully remove the aluminium foil.

Sprinkle over some oregano, and add some crushed nuts.

Fennel Salad with Tuna

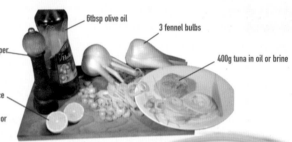

- 6tbsp olive oil
- 3 fennel bulbs
- sat/pepper
- 400g tuna in oil or brine
- 3tbsp lemon juice
- Chopped chives or spring onions

Remove the exterior leaves of the bulbs and **finely chop** the fennel. **Mix them** in a salad bowl with crumbled tuna and olives. **Pour over the sauce** prepared with the ingredients given. **Sprinkle** over the chives. **Mix well,** the salad is tastier after 15mins of soaking. You can replace the tuna with small cubes of ham.

Spicy Fennel with Raisins

Preparation : 15 mins
Cooking : 45 mins

- raisins
- Tomato sauce
- olive oil
- salt/pepper
- coriander, cumin
- sprigs of thyme and bay leaf
- dry white wine
- 4 fennel bulbs
- 10 small onions

Wash the 4 fennel bulbs, **quarter them**. Brown them in some hot oil with about 10 peeled onions. Add salt and pepper, add 1tsp coriander seeds, 1tsp cumin seeds and the sprigs of thyme and bay leaf. Add into the mixture a small pot of tomato sauce, mix with the dry white wine.

Leave to simmer covered for 45mins. Check the seasoning and add a handful of raisins. **Continue cooking for 10mins.**

If the sauce is too liquid, remove the lid and leave to reduce. (can be kept for 2 days in the fridge).

Cabbage

PREPARATION

1 Cut...

2 Remove
leaves...

3 Chop...

remove the base
of the leaves

carefully remove the
leaves one by one

remove the central stalk
of the greenest leaves

cut the cabbage in small
piece or in strips

CABBAGE, KEEPS YOU HEALTHY

Information from the service of nutrition at the Institut Pasteur in Lille.

FACTS ABOUT

CABBAGE

calcium	proteins	carbohydrates	vitamin C	fibres	fats
2 mg	1,4 g	4 g	57 mg	3 g	0,3 g

Average nutritional composition of raw cabbage (for 100g)

ORIGINS AND PRODUCTION

Cabbages originate in Eastern Europe where they grow in the wild on the ocean coast.

Its cultivation started 4000 years ago in Asia (China, Mongolia) and it was pickled for preservation. This type of consumption took over Eastern Europe.

The vegetable was introduced to Britain in the 4th century shortly before the beginning of the Christian era by the Romans.

Cabbages, much liked by Louis XIV, were eaten in the great banquets in France.

Today in Britain, it is grown mainly in the north, east and in the Provence.

It is harvested mainly in Lincolnshire from **October to March**. It is therefore mostly eaten during winter.

NUTRITIONAL QUALITIES

Cabbages are low in calories (23kcal/100g). It actually contains few proteins, carbohydrates and fats.
Its concentration of vitamin C and B9 (folic acid), and fibres are quite high.
It is a vegetable which is quite rich in calcium.

HEALTH BENEFITS

One of the most beneficial reasons for eating cabbage is its vitamin C level, especially when it is eaten raw. This vitamin is an antioxidant and plays a role in the protection against cardiovascular disease and against certain cancers.

The presence of fibres helps regulate intestinal transit.

The calcium content in cabbages adds to the intake of calcium in addition to other dairy products in a healthy balanced diet.

October to March

CHOOSING AND PRESERVING CABBAGES

Fresh cabbages should be chosen if heavy and dense with leaves tightly folded, firm and shiny.
It can be kept simply in the vegetable compartment in the refrigerator where it will be preserved for a week.

Stuffed Cabbage

Preparation : 15 mins
Cooking : 45 mins + 10 mins

- 1 savoy cabbage
- salt/pepper
- 450g minced meat (pork and beef)
- 2 garlic cloves some parsley sprigs
- 1/2 onion

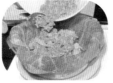

Remove the exterior leaves by cutting the base. Separate the leaves one by one, and then wash them under the tap. **Leave them for 10mins in boiling water to make them 'white'.** Remove them from the water carefully using a small slotted spoon. Place them on a tray. **Roughly cut three leaves.** With the rest garnish the base of a casserole dish. **Let the leaves overhang the edges of the casserole dish.** Mix the chopped cabbage pieces with the minced meat. Add the onion, garlic, and finely chopped parsley. Add salt and pepper. **Knead well together.** Fill the garnished casserole dish with the stuffing. **Fold over the edges of the cabbage leaves and add some more leaves on top.** If possible place a lid on the casserole dish and place in the middle of an oven. You can also cook it in a bain-marie by placing the casserole dish in a pot larger than it filled with a little water, 1 hour on low heat. **Cooking: 45mins at 200°C.** Turn out into a large plate. Garnish with a fresh tomatoe sauce.

Coleslow

Preparation : 10 mins
No cooking

Ingredients

- 300ml single cream
- salt/pepper
- 1/2 onion
- 2tbsp curry powder
- 5 carrots
- 1/4 white cabbage
- Handful of white raisins
- 2tbsp olive oil
- Few drops of Tabasco sauce
- 2tbsp vinegar

Peel the carrots. Cut the white cabbage in large chunks. **Grate the carrots, cabbage and onion in a food processor or by hand.** Mix the single cream with the curry powder, add olive oil and vinegar. Season with salt and pepper. **Add the grated vegetables.** Mix. Adjust the seasoning and gradually add the Tabasco sauce. **Decorate with some raisins.** Place a plate over the mixture and leave to chill for a **few hours in the refrigerator.**

Very easy to ma for an entr and excellent w grilled meat

Cabbage
Hotpot

Preparation : 20 mins
Cooking : 2 h

Ingredients

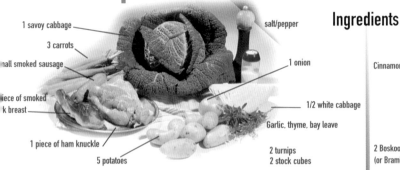

- 1 savoy cabbage
- 3 carrots
- small smoked sausage
- piece of smoked pork breast
- 1 piece of ham knuckle
- 5 potatoes
- salt/pepper
- 1 onion
- 1/2 white cabbage
- Garlic, thyme, bay leave
- 2 turnips
- 2 stock cubes

Remove the large outer leaves of the Savoy cabbage. **Separate the greener leaves and remove the white nerve.** Cut the centre of the cabbage in four. Remove the outer leaves of the **white cabbage** and chop them into large pieces. Wash the cabbages under running tap water. Peel the carrots, potatoes, onions and turnips. Cut the vegetables into large chunks. Put the vegetables **in a large casserole dish.** Add thyme, bay leaf and garlic. Place the meat pieces on top. Season with salt and pepper. Add 1 litre and 1/2 of water and 2 stock cubes.

Cooking: cover the casserole dish and leave to cook on low heat for at **least 2 hours.**

NB: if you are going to serve it the next day, leave to cook again for an hour before serving.

Red Cabbage
with Apples

Preparation : 15 mins
Cooking : 1 h 15 mins + 10 mins

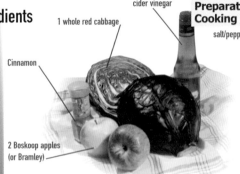

- 1 whole red cabbage
- cider vinegar
- salt/pepper
- Cinnamon
- 2 Boskoop apples (or Bramley)

Cut the cabbage in half. Remove the core, cut into slices. Blanch in a large pot of salted boiling water for 10mins. **Drain and rinse under cold water.** Re-cook covered in salted water for 1 hour. Peel and cut the apples in large chunks.

After 1 hour of cooking remove the cabbage and put it back in the casserole dish with a glass of vinegar. Add the apple pieces, cinnamon and pepper. **Cook for a further 15mins.**

Cabbage
à la Flamande

Ingredients : 1/2 white cabbage 200g diced streaky bacon

Cut the 1/2 cabbage into slices then into smaller pieces. Brown the bacon in a pan **without adding any fat.** When the bacon is slightly melted add the cabbage and then mix. **Leave to cook for 20mins** while mixing from time to time. You can **deglaze** the pan by **adding some water** half-way through cooking.

white beans

PREPARATION

1 Shell...

2 Soak...

1 fresh white beans need
to be shelled

2 dry white beans need
to be soaked

WHITE BEANS, ENERGY PROVIDER

Information from the service of nutrition at the Institut Pasteur in Lille.

white beans

fibres 8 g	vitamin B9 80 µg	iron 2,6 mg	magnesium 50 mg	proteins 7 g	carbohydrates 17 g	potassium 460 mg	fats 0,5 g

Average nutritional composition of cooked white beans (for 100g)

NUTRITIONAL QUALITIES

White beans come from the starchy foods family and they are more legumes than vegetables. Its nutritional composition differs significantly from other green vegetables.

The amount of proteins, carbohydrates and fibres are high whereas the amount of fat is practically zero. However the proteins of legumes are not perfect: this is why it is advised that they should be eaten with other sources of protein such as meat or vegetables.

Calcium, iron, magnesium, phosphorous, potassium and vitamin B9 are present in significant quantities.

ORIGINS AND PRODUCTION

White beans originated in Central America where they were eaten by the Indians.

It wasn't till the 16th century that they appeared in France.

There exist a number of varieties of beans of which there there are butter beans. There are also mange-tout, green beans, runner beans, …

In their dry state, white beans can be found all year round in shops. White beans that need to be shelled are sold after harvest in the months **August to September.**

HEALTH BENEFITS

White beans are rich in proteins which can replace those of meat if they are eaten with dairy products or cereals.

Its high level of fibres regulates intestinal transit.

The amount of iron is equivalent to that of meat. This iron is absorbed well by the body if it is taken at the same time as a food rich in calcium (vegetables and fruits).

CHOOSING AND PRESERVING WHITE BEANS

August to September

Fresh white beans should be chosen firm and brittle. It is possible to dry them yourself in a place which is dry and not too hot.

White beans can be kept in a compartment of the refrigerator, without sealing in a plastic bag to prevent them rotting.

Pesto Soup

Preparation : 15 mins
Cooking : 45 mins

- 2tbsp olive oil
- 3 garlic cloves
- 300g fresh green beans
- 500g of white beans shelled
- parmesan
- 2 or 3 courgettes
- 2 tomatoes
- 5 basil branches
- 2 thyme branches
- 2 or 3 white onions

Trim and rinse the green beans. Cut them in half. **Peel the onions and garlic;** brown them together in a pot with a little oil and thyme. **Roughly peel the courgettes** and cut them in half and then chop into small pieces.

Add chopped tomatoes in to the pot and then the courgettes. Season with salt and pepper. **Add the white beans** and the **green beans. Pour in 1.25 litres of water.** Cover and leave to cook on low heat for about 45mins.

Meanwhile, prepare the pesto.

Preparation of Pesto:
4 garlic cloves, 1 glass of olive oil, 20 fresh basil leaves and 80g grated parmesan.
Peel the garlic and remove the germ. Cut it into small pieces. Finely **chop the basil leaves. Crush the garlic** and add the **basil**. Continue to crush. **Add the oil and the parmesan. Mix** for a few minutes and mash well. Keep in the fridge until serving the soup.

Serve the soup in bowls and add 1 tsp of pesto. Decorate with parmesan shavings and 1 basil leaf.

Mutton with white beans

Preparation : 20 min
Cooking : 1

Ingredients

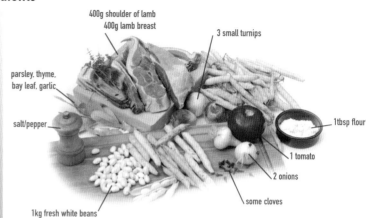

- 400g shoulder of lamb
- 400g lamb breast
- 3 small turnips
- parsley, thyme, bay leaf, garlic
- 1tbsp flour
- salt/pepper
- 1 tomato
- 2 onions
- some cloves
- 1kg fresh white beans

Shell the white beans. **Brown the onions** (cut in half and prick with a clove) with a little butter. **Add the meat.** Season with salt and pepper. Brown for a few minutes. **Sprinkle over the flour, add the thyme, bay leaf and parsley.**

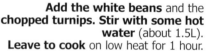

Add the white beans and the **chopped turnips. Stir with some hot water** (about 1.5L). **Leave to cook** on low heat for 1 hour.

White Beans
Courgette and Tuna Salad

Preparation : 10 mins
Cooking : 8 mins
+ 35 mins (fresh white beans)

olive oil

balsamic vinegar

salt/pepper

500g fresh white beans (or tinned white beans)

parsley

1/2 lemon

200g tuna in brine

1 garlic clove

2 courgettes

Preparation: cut the courgettes into round slices and cook them for 8mins in a pot of salted boiling water.

Meanwhile, cook the white beans for 35mins in a large pot of salted boiling water (or drain and rinse the tinned beans).

For the vinaigrette:
2 tbsp olive oil
1tbsp balsamic vinegar
Salt, pepper, juice of half a lemon, a garlic clove crushed, some sprigs of parsley.
Prepare the vinaigrette, then mix with the white beans, tuna and the hot courgettes. Serve warm.

Tip: the tuna can be replaced with about 20 shelled prawns.

white beans
à la Gasconne

Ingredients

Preparation : 10 mins
Cooking : 1 h 15 mins

500g fresh white beans or dried (to be soaked 12h in advance)

2 onions

a knob of butter + a little olive oil

salt/pepper

3 or 4 sausages

2 tomatoes

2 garlic cloves

2 bay leaves

2 sprigs thyme

If using dried white beans: soak them in 1 litre of water **12 hours in advance** and drain them before cooking.

Peel and slice the onions. Brown in a pot with some butter or olive oil. When the onions start to colour **add the roughly chopped tomatoes**.

Add peeled garlic, mix. Add the thyme and bay leaves. **Add the white beans. Stir, season with salt and pepper.** Place in the sausages and pour in 1 litre of water.

Cover and leave to cook on low heat for 1h15mins. Serve hot (the cooking of fresh white beans is quicker: 45mins).

Potatoes

PREPARATION

1 Peel...

1

2 Cut...

2

in fine slices or chunks. It can also be cut lengthways
or in small cubes.

POTATOES, CARBOHYDRATES FOR ENERGY!

Information from the service of nutrition at the Institut Pasteur in Lille.

POTATOES

| energy 81 kcal | proteins 1,5 g | carbohydrates 18 g | vitamin C 9 mg | magnesium 50 mg |

Average nutritional composition of boiled potatoes (for 100g)

ORIGINS AND PRODUCTION

Potatoes come from the Cordillera of Andes where it was eaten by the Incas under the name of 'papa' 1000 year BC.

They were introduced to Europe via Spain in 16th century and arrived in Britain around the 1590s.

There exists more than 3000 varieties of potatoes but not all are eaten. In the shops, two categories are sold: the maincrop and new potatoes.

Each type is grown at different times of the year: new potatoes are planted in January to March and harvested 3 months later, maincrops are planted in between March and May and harvested from September to October.

There are numerous varieties of potatoes. The size, form, texture of the flesh and even colour can be used to distinguish them.

The most common types in Britain are: Jersey Royal, King Edward, Maris Piper, Desiree, Cara…

NUTRITIONAL QUALITIES

Potatoes are richer in carbohydrates (20%) than other vegetables, which is why it is classified as part of the starchy foods family. However it contain few proteins and no fats. It has a high concentration of vitamin C, potassium and magnesium.
It is the leading source of polyphenols along with apples in the British diet.

HEALTH BENEFITS

One of the main benefits of the potato is its contribution to fulfilling the need for vitamin C, even when it is cooked. This is better preserved when the potatoes are cooked with their skin.

Of course, like all vegetables, it is low in fat. The cooking method should be varied as some types, such as frying, can increase the amount of fat.

Eaten in salads (cold) it has a lower glycaemic index.

CHOOSING AND PRESERVING POTATOES

Potatoes should be chosen firm, unblemished with no roots and without green patches.
They should be kept in a cool, dark and well-ventilated place to prevent them form going green.
Potatoes with firm flesh are ideal for cooking peeled, steamed or sautéed.
Other potatoes are usually used to make purees, oven-cooking or chips.

Potato Salad with Capers

Preparation : 15 mins
Cooking : 10 mins

Ingredients

- 1tsp mustard
- 1 small jar of capers in vinegar
- Sel / poivre
- 1 new onion
- 500g firm potatoes (mostly small)
- 2 boiled eggs
- 2tbsp oil

Cook the potatoes whole and unpeeled **for 10mins** (after removing any earth under running tap water) in a **pot of salted boiling water**. Refresh them quickly under cold water. Boil the eggs in water for 6mins.

Peel the potatoes and cut them in **large round slices.** Peel and chop the onion. add them to the potatoes. **Add in the jar of capers** (with half of the vinegar).

Add the mustard mixed with the oil to the potatoes. Season with pepper. **Mix without crushing** the potatoes. Shell the eggs and cut into round slices; add to the potatoes.

Chill in the refrigerator for at least 1 hour covered with cling film.

You can also add some tuna pieces in oil (in which case do not add the oil in the seasoning) and some basil leaves.

Potatoes with Milk and Tarragon

Preparation : 10 mins
Cooking : 8 mins

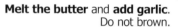

- 6 medium potatoes
- 250ml milk
- Some sprigs of tarragon
- 25g butter
- salt/pepper
- Grated nutmeg
- 1 medium onion
- 6 garlic cloves

Peel and wash the potatoes. **Cut** them in round slices of about 3 mm thickness. Dry the slices on absorbent paper. **Peel the garlic** and remove the germ. Chop into small pieces. **Peel and chop the onion.**

Melt the butter and **add garlic**. Do not brown.

After 1 minute, **add the potatoes.** Mix, add pepper and sprinkle with grated nutmeg. Mix and a leave on low heat for a few minutes. Season with salt. **Pick the leaves of the tarragon** and cut them if they are too large. Add them to the potatoes. Leave to cook for a few more minutes.

Pour in the milk and stir to allow it to be soaked up by the potatoes. **Leave covered and on low heat for 8 minutes**. Serve immediately. This dish is a ideal accompaniment to grilled veal ribs, with a lightly seasoned green salad.

Potato and Apple Gratin

Ingredients

- 100ml low fat crème fraîche + milk (optional)
- salt/pepper
- large potatoes
- 50g grated gruyere
- 3 apples (granny smith)
- Grated nutmeg
- 2 thyme sprigs
- 1 medium onion

eel the potatoes. **Peel and quarter the apples** and core them.
t the potatoes with the help of a food processor to achieve perfect
und slices. **Wipe the potatoes slices** with absorbent paper.
t the apples into fine slices and leave
em separately in a dish.

t **the peeled onions** in the same way.
a buttered deep sided oven-proof dish
read a layer of potatoes followed by
ayer of apples and finish with a layer
potatoes. Season each layer with salt
d pepper. **On each potato layer**
rinkle over some nutmeg. Add
me

oonfuls of **crème fraîche** halfway
ough and on the top layer.

rinkle over some **grated gruyere** on
e top and **bake for 1h at 190°C**.
over with aluminium foil the first 30mins
cooking).

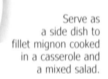

Serve as
a side dish to
fillet mignon cooked
in a casserole and
a mixed salad.

Potato Puree

Simple!

- 150ml milk
- salt/pepper
- 1.5kg potatoes
- 1tsp butter (optional)

Peel the 1.5kg of potatoes.
Cut into large chunks.
Boil them in a large pot
of boiling salted water for 15mins.
Drain the potatoes.

Mash with a potato masher
or puree maker and
add the milk.
When they are mashed,
add **a little knob of butter.**
You can also add some pepper
and some grated nutmeg.

Index
Recipes are for 4 people

The authors would like to thank: Johan Sobry, The Deswarte farm in Ghyvelde (59),
Le Potager des Princes (Chantilly (60)), Anne Selliez for her hospitality,
the Institut Pasteur of Lille, the gardeners of Auray.

For Adele, Lucas and Colin, the new amateurs of vegetables…